SPIRITUAL
LEADERSHIP

SPIRITUAL LEADERSHIP

by

J. OSWALD SANDERS

Consulting Director
Overseas Missionary Fellowship

MOODY PRESS
CHICAGO

© 1967, 1980 by
THE MOODY BIBLE INSTITUTE
OF CHICAGO

Revised Edition

All Scripture quotations, except those noted otherwise, are from the *New American Standard Bible,* © 1960, 1962, 1963, 1968, 1971, 1972, 1973, 1975, and 1977 by The Lockman Foundation, and are used by permission.

The use of selected references from various versions of the Bible in this publication does not necessarily imply publisher endorsement of the versions in their entirety.

Library of Congress Cataloging in Publication Data

Sanders, John Oswald, 1902-
Spiritual leadership.

Includes bibliographical references and indexes.
1. Christian leadership.   I. Title.

BV652.1.S3   1980   253'.2   80-21415

ISBN 0-8024-8221-X

13 14 15 16 Printing/LC/Year 92 91 90 89 88 87

Printed in the United States of America

CONTENTS

PREFACE TO THE FIRST EDITION

This book has grown out of two series of messages delivered to the leaders of the Overseas Missionary Fellowship at conferences in Singapore in 1964 and 1966. It was then suggested that these messages should be amplified and shared with a wider public. The author has acceded to this request.

The principles of leadership in both the temporal and spiritual realms are presented and illustrated from both Scripture and the biographies of eminent men of God. Not every reader will have access to many of the biographies from which these illustrations are drawn, and this has encouraged the author to include pertinent incidents from the lives of men whose leadership has been more than usually successful. Wherever possible, sources are indicated. In the case of Scripture references, that translation has been used which appeared to the author to be most accurate and luminous.

The material has been presented in a form that is calculated to be of help even to younger Christians in whose hearts the Holy Spirit is working to create a holy ambition to place all their powers at the disposal of the Redeemer. If there is something, too, that will rekindle aspiration and crystallize a fresh purpose in the hearts of those further along the road of leadership, the aim of the book will be realized.

PREFACE TO THE REVISED EDITION

The reception accorded to *Spiritual Leadership* in its American, British, Chinese, and German editions, has encouraged me to revise and enlarge it. The fact that it has been widely used around the world as required reading in colleges, missionary societies, and other Christian organizations indicates the possibility of continuing usefulness. Translation rights into other languages have been granted, an indication that it is relevant to cultures other than our own.

Two extra chapters have been added—"The Master's Master Principle" and "Improving Leadership Potential," as well as some new material to other chapters where it seemed desirable.

This edition is issued in the hope that it may continue to make a contribution to the church in the area of spiritual leadership.

I humble myself
I bring me low
down to my knees
to serve
to love
to sacrifice

I seek nothing for myself
I am all for

God

everything is for

(God)

♡
†
I love You Lord

1

AN HONORABLE AMBITION

To aspire to leadership is an honourable ambition.

1 TIMOTHY 3:1, NEB*

Are you seeking great things for yourself? Do not seek them.

JEREMIAH 45:5

Paul's affirmation that aspiration to leadership is an honorable ambition will not be accepted by all Christians without a measure of reservation. Should it not be the office that seeks the man, rather than the man the office? Is it not perilous to put an ambitious man into office? Is there not more than a modicum of truth in the claim that ambition is "the last infirmity of noble minds"? Was not Shakespeare expressing a profound truth when he made Wolsey say:

> Cromwell, I charge thee, fling away ambitions,
> By that sin fell the angels; how can man then,
> The image of his Maker, hope to profit by't?

*New English Bible.

I hunger for You Jesus
I am so desperate

We cannot deny that there is an ambition that warrants those strictures. But there are ambitions that are noble and worthy and to be cherished. When the two passages at the head of this chapter are held in constant tension by one who desires to be effective in the service of God and realize the highest potential of his life, there need be little fear for the outcome of that ambition.

In appraising the honorable ambition of which Paul speaks, several factors must be kept in mind. We are apt to view his categorical statement in the light of the honor and prestige that in our day accrue to those in positions of Christian leadership. When Paul wrote, however, conditions were much different. Then the office of bishop, or overseer, far from being a coveted, easy position, often involved great dangers and heavy responsibilities. Not infrequently hardship, contempt, and rejection were its rewards. In times of persecution the leader drew the fire, and he was the first to suffer.

When read in the light of those conditions, Paul's statement does not seem so filled with danger as might at first appear. Mere place-seekers and charlatans would have little heart for such an onerous assignment. Under those discouraging circumstances, Paul felt it right and necessary to provide some incentive to leadership and to give a word of praise to those who were willing to incur the risks involved. Hence his statement: "To aspire to leadership is an honourable ambition."

That very situation is repeated today. It was the

leaders of the church in China who suffered most at the hands of the Communists. It was the pastor of the Little Flock in Nepal who suffered years of imprisonment, while his church members were released early. In many countries even today, spiritual leadership is no sinecure.

It should be observed that it is not the *office* of overseer but the *function* of overseeing that Paul asserts is honorable and noble. It is the most privileged work in the world, and its glorious character should be an incentive to covet it because, when sought from highest motives, it yields both present and eternal dividends. In Paul's times, only deep love for Christ and genuine concern for His church would provide men with a sufficiently powerful motive to aspire to that office. But in most lands today Christian leadership confers prestige and privilege; and unworthy ambition may easily induce self-seeking and unspiritual men to covet office.

It is that very fact that makes Jeremiah's counsel to Baruch so pertinent: "Seekest thou great things for thyself? seek them not" (KJV†). He is not warning against ambition per se, but against *self-centered* ambition—"great things *for thyself.*" A desire to be great is not necessarily in itself sinful. It is the motivation that determines its character. Our Lord did not discount or disparage aspiration to greatness, but He did pointedly expose and stigmatize unworthy motivation.

All Christians are under obligation to make the

†King James Version.

most of their lives, to develop to the utmost their God-given powers and capacities. But Jesus taught that any ambition that centers on and terminates on one-self is wrong. In an address to ordinands, Bishop Stephen Neill had this to say: "I am inclined to think that ambition in any ordinary sense of the term is nearly always sinful in ordinary men. I am certain that in the Christian it is always sinful, and that it is most inexcusable of all in the ordained minister."[1]

On the other hand, an ambition that has as its center the glory of God and the welfare of His church is not only legitimate, but is also positively praise-worthy.

Our word *ambition* derives from a Latin word meaning "canvassing for promotion." A variety of ingredients may be present in ambition—to be seen and approved by men, to be popular, to stand well among one's contemporaries, to exercise control over others. Ambitious men enjoy the power that money or authority brings. Such carnal ambitions were roundly rebuked by the Lord. The true spiritual leader will never canvass for promotion.

To His ambitious disciples Jesus announced a new standard of greatness: "You know that those who are recognized as rulers of the Gentiles lord it over them; and their great men exercise authority over them. But it is not so [or, to be the case] among you, but who-ever wishes to be great among you shall be your ser-vant, and whoever wishes to be first among you shall be slave of all" (Mark 10:42-44). We shall consider that incident in greater detail in a later chapter.

At the beginning of any study of spiritual leadership, it is essential that the divinely-enunciated master principle be clearly understood and firmly embraced. True greatness, true leadership, is achieved not by reducing men to one's service but in giving oneself in selfless service to them. And that is never done without cost. It involves drinking a bitter cup and experiencing a painful baptism of suffering. The true spiritual leader is concerned infinitely more with the service he can render God and his fellowmen than with the benefits and pleasures he can extract from life. He aims to put more into life than he takes out of it.

"One of the outstanding ironies of history is the utter disregard of ranks and titles in the final judgments men pass on each other," said Samuel Brengle. "The final estimate of men shows that history cares not an iota for the rank or title a man has borne, or the office he has held, but only the quality of his deeds and the character of his mind and heart."[2]

"Let it once be fixed that a man's ambition is to fit into God's plan for him, and he has a North Star ever in sight to guide him steadily over any sea, however shoreless it seems," wrote S. D. Gordon. "He has a compass that points true in the thickest fog and fiercest storm, and regardless of magnetic rocks."

Although Count Zinzendorf was strongly drawn to classical pursuits and tempted by rank and riches, his attitude and ambition were summed up in one sentence: "I have one passion; it is He, He alone." He renounced selfish ambition and became the renowned founder and leader of the Moravian church. His followers drank deeply of the spirit of their leader and circled the world with the gospel. Their missionary activity had the unique distinction, in days when missionary work was on a very limited scale, of bringing into being an overseas church with three times as many communicants as in their home churches. One member out of every ninety-two became a foreign missionary.

> Because we children of Adam want to become
>   great,
>   He became small.
> Because we will not stoop,
>   He humbled Himself.
> Because we want to rule,
>   He came to serve.

NOTES

1. Stephen Neill, "Address to Ordinands," *The Record*, 28 March 1947, p. 161.
2. C. W. Hall, *Samuel Logan Brengle* (New York: Salvation Army, 1933), p. 274.

2

THE SEARCH FOR LEADERS

For not from the east, nor from the west, nor from the desert comes exaltation; but God is the Judge; He puts down one, and exalts another.

Give me a man of God—one man,
   Whose faith is master of his mind,
And I will right all wrongs
   And bless the name of all mankind.

Give me a man of God—one man,
   Whose tongue is touched with heaven's fire,
And I will flame the darkest hearts
   With high resolve and clean desire.

Give me a man of God—one man,
   One mighty prophet of the Lord,
And I will give you peace on earth,
   Bought with a prayer and not a sword.

Give me a man of God—one man,
  True to the vision that he sees,
And I will build your broken shrines
  And bring the nations to their knees.

                              GEORGE LIDDELL

God and man are constantly searching for leaders
in the various branches of Christian enterprise. In
the Scriptures, God is frequently represented as
searching for a man of a certain type. Not men, but
a man. Not a group, but an individual.

"The LORD has sought out for Himself *a man* after
his own heart" (1 Sam. 13:14, italics added).

"I looked, and behold, there was *no man*" (Jer. 4:
25, italics added).

"Run ye to and fro through the streets of Jerusalem, and see . . . if ye can find *a man* . . . that exe-
cuteth judgment, that seeketh the truth; and I will
pardon it" (Jer. 5:1, KJV, italics added).

"I searched for *a man* . . . who should . . . stand in
the gap before Me for the land" (Ezek. 22:30, italics
added).

Both Scripture and the history of Israel and the
church attest that when God does discover a man who
conforms to His spiritual requirement, who is willing
to pay the full price of discipleship, He uses him to
the limit, despite his patent shortcomings. Such men
were Moses, Gideon and David, Martin Luther, John
Wesley, Adoniram Judson, William Carey, and a host
of others.

The supernatural nature of the church demands a

leadership that rises above the human. And yet, has there ever been a greater dearth of God-anointed and God-mastered men to meet that crucial need? In a sense it has always been true that that type of dedicated leadership has been in short supply, for the simple reason that its demands are too stringent.

"The Church is painfully in need of leaders," lamented William E. Sangster. "I wait to hear a voice and no voice comes. I love the back seat in Synod and Conference. I would always rather listen than speak—but there is no clarion voice to listen to."[1]

The overriding need of the church, if it is to discharge its obligation to the rising generation, is for a leadership that is authoritative, spiritual, and sacrificial. *Authoritative,* because people love to be led by one who knows where he is going and who inspires confidence. They follow almost without question the man who shows himself wise and strong, who adheres to what he believes. *Spiritual,* because a leadership that is unspiritual, that can be fully explained in terms of the natural, although ever so attractive and competent, will result only in sterility and moral and spiritual bankruptcy. *Sacrificial,* because modeled on the life of the One who gave Himself a sacrifice for the whole world, who left us an example that we should follow His steps.

The church has always prospered most when it has been blessed with strong, spiritual leaders who expected and experienced the touch of the supernatural in their service. The lack of such men is a symptom of the malaise that has gripped it. The clarion voices that used to make the pulpit the paramount influence in the land are tragically few. In a world aflame, the voice of the church has sunk to a pathetic whisper. It is the binding duty of those in positions of leadership to face up to the situation and do all in their power to see that the torch of a truly spiritual leadership is passed on to the younger men.

Leadership is often viewed as the product of natural endowments and traits of personality—intellectual capacity, force of will, enthusiasm. That such talents and scholastic attainments do greatly enhance leadership is beyond question, but those are not the factors of paramount importance in the spiritual leader. "The real qualities of leadership are to be found in those who are willing to suffer for the sake of objectives great enough to demand their wholehearted obedience."

Spiritual leaders are not made by election or appointment, by men or any combination of men, nor by conferences or synods. Only God can make them. Simply holding a position of importance does not constitute one a leader, nor do taking courses in leadership, or resolving to become a leader. The only method is that of *qualifying* to be a leader. Religious position can be conferred by bishops and boards, but not spiritual authority, which is the prime essential of Christian leadership. That comes—often unsought— to those who in earlier life have proved themselves worthy of it by spirituality, discipline, ability, and diligence, men who have heeded the command: "Do you seek great things for yourself? Do not seek them," and instead have sought first the kingdom of God. Spiritual leadership is a thing of the Spirit and is conferred by God alone. When His searching eye alights on a man who has qualified, He anoints him with His Spirit and separates him to his distinctive ministry (Acts 9:17; 22:21).

Samuel Logan Brengle was one of the truly great leaders of the Salvation Army. A man of scholarship as well as of singular spiritual power, he outlined the road to spiritual authority and leadership in challenging words:

> It is not won by promotion, but by many prayers and tears. It is attained by confessions of sin, and much heartsearching and humbling before God; by self-surrender, a courageous sacrifice of every idol, a bold, deathless, uncompromising and uncomplaining embracing of the cross, and by an eternal, unfaltering looking unto Jesus crucified. It is not gained by seeking great things for ourselves, but rather, like Paul, by counting those things that are gain to us as loss for Christ. That is a great price, but it must be unflinchingly paid by him who would be not merely a nominal but a real spiritual leader of men, a leader whose power is recognized and felt in heaven, on earth and in hell.[2]

That is the type of man for whom God is searching, on whose behalf He desires to show Himself strong (2 Chron. 16:9). But not all who aspire to leadership are willing to pay so exacting a price. However, God's conditions must be complied with in secret before He will honor a man in public. Our Lord made clear to James and John that there is a sovereignty about leadership in His kingdom. The highest positions are reserved for those who have qualified in secret. It is that element of sovereignty that begets awe and a great humility in those to whom leadership is entrusted.

It remains to be said that there can be such a thing as inverted leadership. If those in positions of power and influence fail to lead their people into the spiritual uplands, they will unconsciously yet nonetheless surely lead them down into the lowlands, for none can live to himself.

> Give me men to match my mountains,
>   Give me men to match my plains,
> Men with empires in their purpose,
>   Men with eras in their brains.

AUTHOR UNKNOWN

NOTES

1. Paul E. Sangster, *Doctor Sangster* (London: Epworth, 1962), p. 109.
2. Samuel Logan Brengle, *The Soul-Winner's Secret* (London: Salvation Army, 1918), p. 22.

3

THE MASTER'S MASTER PRINCIPLE

Whoever wishes to become great among you shall be your servant; and whoever wishes to be first among you shall be slave of all.

MARK 10:43-44

In the light of the tremendous stress laid upon the leadership role in both secular and religious worlds, it is surprising to discover that in the King James Version of the Bible, for example, the term "leader" occurs only six times, three times in the singular and three in the plural. That is not to say that the theme is not prominent in the Bible, but it is usually referred to in different terms, the most prominent being "servant." It is not "Moses, my leader," but "Moses, my servant." That emphasis is consonant with Christ's teaching on the subject.[1]

Although Jesus was not a revolutionary in the political sense, many of His teachings were startling and revolutionary, and none more so than those on leadership. In the contemporary world, the term *servant* has a very lowly connotation, but that was not so as Jesus used it. Indeed, He elevated it, equating it with greatness, and that was certainly a revolutionary concept. Most of us would have no objection to being masters, but servanthood holds little attraction.

Christ's view of His kingdom was that of a community of members serving one another—*mutual service*. Paul advocates the same idea: "Through love serve one another" (Gal. 5:13). And of course our loving service is to spread to the needy world around us. But in the life of the church today, it is usually the few who serve the many.

Jesus well knew that such an other-worldly concept would not be welcomed by a self-pleasing world of men. But nothing less than that was what he required of those who desired to rise to leadership in His kingdom.

The contrast between the world's idea of leadership and that of Christ is brought into sharp focus in Mark 10:42-43: "You know that those who are recognized as rulers of the Gentiles lord it over them; and their great men exercise authority over them. *But it is not* [*to be*] *so among you*. But whoever wishes to become great among you shall be your servant; and whoever wishes to be first among you shall be slave of all" (italics added).

It was a lesson James and John had not mastered. They had, however, taken seriously the Master's promise "Truly I say to you, that you who have followed Me, in the regeneration when the Son of Man will sit on His glorious throne, you also shall sit upon twelve thrones, judging the twelve tribes of Israel" (Matt. 19:28). In selfish ambition they used their doting mother in an endeavor to forestall their colleagues and preempt the prime positions in the coming kingdom.

But Jesus would have none of it. There must be no lobbying for office. "You do not know what you are asking for," was the reply. Nor did they. They wanted the glory, but not the shame; the crown, but not the cross; to be masters, not servants.

Their request afforded Jesus the occasion to present two leadership principles of permanent relevance.

● *There is a sovereignty in spiritual leadership.*

"To sit on My right [hand] or on My left, this is not Mine to give; but it is for *those for whom it has been prepared*" (Mark 10:40, italics added).

Our emphasis would probably have been, "It is for those who have prepared themselves for it." But Jesus emphasized the fundamental difference in leadership principles. "It is not so among you." Places of spiritual ministry and leadership are sovereignly assigned by God. The *Good News Bible* translation of verse 40 is: "It is God who will give these places to those for whom He has prepared them."

No theological training or leadership course will automatically confer spiritual leadership or qualify one for an effective ministry. Jesus was later to tell them, "You did not choose Me, but I chose you, and appointed you" (John 15:16). To be able to affirm,

"I am not here by selection of a man or the election of a group, but by the sovereign appointment of God," gives great confidence to the Christian worker.

• *There is suffering involved in spiritual leadership.*

"Are you able to drink the cup that I drink, or to be baptized with the baptism with which I am baptized?" (Mark 10:38).

Jesus was too straightforward and honest to conceal the cost in the service of the kingdom. For the fulfillment of the stupendous task entrusted to Him, He needed men and women of quality with eyes wide open, who would follow Him to the death.

To the Lord's probing question, they returned the glib answer "We are able"—thus betraying a tragic lack of self-knowledge. Jesus told them that they would indeed drink the cup and experience the baptism. They must learn that for an influential spiritual ministry there would be a steep price to pay—and that it cannot be paid in a lump sum. In the end, it cost James his head, and John finished his days in a concentration camp.

They desired to attain leadership "on the cheap," but Jesus' words soon disillusioned them. The fundamental lessons that *greatness comes only by way of servanthood,* and that first place in leadership is gained only by becoming *everybody's slave,* must have come as a great and unwelcome shock.

It is noteworthy that only once did Jesus say that He was leaving His disciples an example, and that was when He washed their feet (John 13:15)—an example of *servanthood.* And only once did any other writer say that He had left an example—and that was an example of suffering (1 Pet. 2:21). Thus the thoughts of suffering and servanthood are linked, even as they were in the life of the Lord. And is the servant greater than his Lord?

In stating that primacy in leadership comes by way of primacy in servanthood, Jesus did not have in mind mere *acts of service,* for those can be performed from very dubious motives. He meant the *spirit of servanthood,* which He expressed when He claimed, "I am among you as He that serves."

Isaiah 42:1-5, a Messianic passage, reveals what the spirit of servanthood means, and outlines in this prophetic foreview the features that would qualify the coming Messiah as the ideal Servant of the Lord.

Israel had been chosen by God to be His servant through whom He could reveal Himself to the world. But the nation failed Him dismally at every turn. However, where Israel failed, Jesus succeeded gloriously, and the principles of His life must be the pattern for ours.

Here are some of those principles:

DEPENDENCE

"Behold My Servant whom I uphold" (v. 1), a statement with Messianic significance. In fulfilling this prophetic intimation, Jesus voluntarily "emptied Himself" (Phil. 2:7), surrendering His privileges and the independent exercise of His will. Though possessing all the powers and prerogatives of deity, He voluntarily became dependent upon His Father. Though

He upheld "all things by the word of His power" (Heb. 1:3), so fully did He identify Himself with the sinless infirmities of our humanity, that in His manhood He Himself needed to be upheld. That divine paradox is one of the staggering aspects of Christ's condescension. In the measure in which we adopt the same attitude will the Holy Spirit be able to use us.

APPROVAL

"My chosen one in whom My soul delights" (v. 1). The delight of Jehovah in His ideal Servant was warmly reciprocated, for in another Messianic reference the Son says, "I delight to do Thy will, O my God" (Psalm 40:8).

MODESTY

"He will not cry out or raise His voice, nor make His voice heard in the street" (v. 2). The ministry of God's Servant would not be strident and flamboyant, but modest and self-effacing. In this day of blatant and arrogant self-advertisement, that is a most desirable quality.

The devil tempted Jesus on that point when he challenged Him to create a stir by making a miraculous leap from the parapet of the Temple. But He did not fall to the tempter's wile.

God's Servant works so quietly and unobtrusively that many even doubt His existence. His method justifies the statement "Thou art a God who hides Himself" (Isa. 45:15). It is recorded of the cherubim, those angelic servants of the Lord, that they used four of their six wings to conceal their faces and their feet—a graphic representation of contentment with hidden service (Isa. 6:2).

EMPATHY

"A bruised reed He will not break, and a dimly burning wick He will not extinguish" (v. 3). The Lord's Servant would be sympathetic and understanding with the weak and erring. Failing men and women are often crushed under the callous tread of their fellowmen; but not so with the ideal Servant. He was to specialize in mending bruised reeds and fanning the smoking wick into a flame.

Many, even Christian workers, ignore those who have failed and "pass by on the other side." They want a ministry more rewarding and more worthy of their powers—something more spectacular than bearing with the relapses and backslidings of frail humanity; but it is a noble work to reclaim those whom the world despises. How dimly Peter's wick burned in the judgment hall, but what a brilliant flame blazed on the day of Pentecost! His interview with God's ideal Servant put everything right.

OPTIMISM

"He will not be disheartened or crushed, until He has established justice in the earth" (v. 4). God's Servant would be undiscourageable. A pessimist never makes an inspiring leader. Hope and optimism are essential qualities for the servant of God as he battles with the powers of darkness for the souls of men.

God's Servant would be optimistic until His full objective is attained.

ANOINTING

"I have put My Spirit upon Him" (v. 1). By themselves, the preceding five qualities would be insufficient for His tremendous task. A touch of the supernatural was required, and that was supplied in the anointing of the Spirit. "You know of Jesus of Nazareth, how God anointed Him with the Holy Spirit and with power, and how He went about doing good" (Acts 10:38).

The same anointing that God's ideal Servant received is available for us. Until the Spirit descended upon Him at His baptism, Jesus created no stir in Nazareth, but then events of world-shaking importance began to happen. Is the servant greater than his lord? Can we dispense with that which was the prime essential for the effectiveness of His ministry on earth?

NOTES

1. Paul S. Rees, "The Community Clue," *Life of Faith*, 26 September 1976, p. 3.

4

NATURAL AND SPIRITUAL LEADERSHIP

When I came to you . . . my message and my preaching were not in persuasive words of wisdom, but in demonstration of the Spirit and of power.

1 CORINTHIANS 2:1, 4

Leadership is influence, the ability of one person to influence others. One man can lead others only to the extent that he can influence them to follow his lead. That fact is supported by definitions of leadership by men who have themselves wielded great influence.

From among military leaders, Lord Montgomery defines it in these terms: "Leadership is the capacity and will to rally men and women to a common purpose, and the character which inspires confidence."[1] Sir Winston Churchill was an outstanding exemplar of that quality.

Fleet Admiral Nimitz said, "Leadership may be defined as that quality in a leader that inspires sufficient confidence in his subordinates as to be willing to accept his views and carry out his commands."

General Charles Gordon once asked Li Hung Chang, an old Chinese leader, a double question: "What is leadership? And how is humanity divided?" He received this cryptic answer: "There are only three kinds of people in the world—those that are immovable, those that are movable, and those that move them!"

In the religious realm, John R. Mott, a world leader in student circles, gave as his definition, "A leader is a man who knows the road, who can keep ahead, and who pulls others after him."[2] P. T. Chandapilla, an Indian student leader, defines Christian leadership as a vocation where there is a perfect blending of qualities that are both human and divine, or a harmonized working of God and man, given over to the ministry and blessing of other people.

From the political angle, President Truman's definition was: "A leader is a person who has the ability to get others to do what they don't want to do, and like it."

Spiritual leadership is a blending of natural and spiritual qualities. Even the natural qualities are not self-produced but God-given, and therefore reach their highest effectiveness when employed in the service of God and for His glory. The definitions above concern leadership in general. Although spiritual leadership partakes of those qualities, there are other elements that supplement and take precedence over them. Personality is a prime factor in natural leadership. "The degree of influence will depend on the personality of the man," wrote Lord Montgomery, "the 'incandescence' of which he is capable, the flame which burns within him, the magnetism which will draw the hearts of men towards him."[3]

The spiritual leader, however, influences others not by the power of his own personality alone but by that personality irradiated, interpenetrated, and empowered by the Holy Spirit. Because he permits the Holy Spirit undisputed control of his life, the Spirit's power can flow unhindered through him to others.

Spiritual leadership is a matter of superior spiritual power, and that can never be self-generated. There is no such thing as a self-made spiritual leader. He is able to influence others spiritually only because the Spirit is able to work in and through him to a greater degree than in those whom he leads.

It is a general principle that we can influence and lead others only so far as we ourselves have gone. The person most likely to be successful is one who leads not by merely pointing the way but by having trodden it himself. We are leaders to the extent that we inspire others to follow us.

At a large gathering of Protestant missions leaders in China, the question of qualifications for leadership was being discussed. There was vigorous debate on the subject. D. E. Hoste, general director of the China Inland Mission, sat quietly listening until the chairman asked if he had anything to say on the subject. From all over the auditorium came murmurs of approval at the invitation, for his contributions to a discussion were always listened to with more than ordinary interest.

With a twinkle in his eye, he said in his curiously high-pitched voice: "It occurs to me that perhaps the best test of whether one is a qualified leader, is to find out whether anyone is following him."[4]

BORN OR MADE?

To the question "Are leaders born or made," there have been a variety of answers. It would appear that the correct answer is, "Both." Leadership has been defined as an "elusive and electric quality" that comes directly from God. On the other hand, it is clear that leadership skills can be cultivated and developed. Each of us from birth possesses skills that either qualify or disqualify us for certain tasks. Those skills often lie dormant until some crisis calls forth their exercise. They can and should be developed.

Some appear to attain leadership purely by reason of a series of fortuitous circumstances. They happened to be available at the crucial moment, and no one better qualified was on the horizon. But closer investigation will usually reveal that the selection was not accidental. Behind the scenes a hidden training had been taking place in the life of the person involved that fitted him for the position. Joseph was a perfect example of that. His elevation to prime minister of Egypt seemed to be purely fortuitous, but in fact it was the outcome of thirteen years of rigorous though hidden training under the hand of God.

Natural leadership and spiritual leadership have many points of similarity, but there are some respects in which they may be antithetical. That is seen when some of their dominant characteristics are set over against one another.

Natural	*Spiritual*
Self-confident	Confident in God
Knows men	Also knows God
Makes own decisions	Seeks to find God's will
Ambitious	Self-effacing
Originates own methods	Finds and follows God's methods
Enjoys commanding others	Delights to obey God
Motivated by personal considerations	Motivated by love for God and man
Independent	God-dependent

Although conversion does not normally make leaders of people who would never become such otherwise, church history teaches that in the hour of full surrender the Holy Spirit sometimes releases gifts and qualities that have long remained dormant. It is the prerogative of the Spirit to bestow spiritual gifts that greatly enhance the leadership potential of the recipient.

This was Dr. A. W. Tozer's conviction:

> A true and safe leader is likely to be one who has no desire to lead, but is forced into a position of leadership by the inward pressure of the Holy Spirit and the press of external situation. Such were Moses and David and the Old

Testament prophets. I think there was hardly
a great leader from Paul to the present day but
was drafted by the Holy Spirit for the task, and
commissioned by the Lord of the Church to fill
a position he had little heart for. I believe it
might be accepted as a fairly reliable rule of
thumb that the man who is ambitious to lead is
disqualified as a leader. The true leader will
have no desire to lord it over God's heritage,
but will be humble, gentle, self-sacrificing and
altogether as ready to follow as to lead, when the
Spirit makes it clear that a wiser and more gifted
man than himself has appeared.[5]

In the biography of William E. Sangster, a private
manuscript found after his death illustrates that contention. He was writing of his growing conviction
that he should take more part in the leadership of the
Methodist church in England.

This is the will of God for me. I did not
choose it. I sought to escape it. But it has come.
Something else has come too. A sense of cer-
tainty that God does not want me only for a
preacher. He wants me also for a leader—a
leader in Methodism.
I feel a commissioning to work under God for
the revival of this branch of His Church—care-
less of my own reputation; indifferent to the
comments of older and jealous men.
I am thirty-six. If I am to serve God in this
way, I must no longer shrink from the task—
but *do* it.
I have examined my heart for ambition. I am

> certain it is not there. I hate the criticism I shall evoke and the painful chatter of people. Obscurity, quiet browsing among books, and the service of simple people is my taste—but by the will of God, this is my task. God help me.
>
> Bewildered and unbelieving, I hear the voice of God say to me: "I want to sound the note through you." O God, did ever an apostle shrink from his task more? I dare not say "No" but, like Jonah, I would fain run away.[6]

That spiritual leadership and authority cannot be explained solely on the grounds of natural ability is strikingly exemplified in the life of Saint Francis of Assisi. On one occasion Brother Masseo, looking earnestly at Francis, began to say: "Why thee? Why thee?" He repeated it again and again as if to mock him.

"What are you saying?" cried Francis at last.

"I am saying that everybody follows thee, everyone desires to see thee, hear thee, obey thee, and yet for all that, thou are neither beautiful, nor learned, nor of noble family. Whence comes it that it should be thee whom the world desires to follow?"

When Francis heard those words, he was filled with joy, raised his eyes to heaven and, after remaining a long time absorbed in contemplation, knelt praising and blessing God with extraordinary fervor. Then he turned to Brother Masseo.

> "Thou wishest to know? It is because the eyes of the Most High have willed it so. He continually watches the good and the wicked,

and as His most holy eyes have not found among
sinners any smaller man, nor any more insufficient and sinful, therefore He has chosen me to
accomplish the marvelous work which God hath
undertaken; He chose me because He could find
none more worthless, and He wished to con-
found the nobility and grandeur, the strength,
the beauty and the learning of this world."[7]

Much may be learned from the wisdom of men who
have made their mark as leaders. Two men already
quoted had tests by which they determined the leadership potential of men they were interviewing.

Lord Montgomery enunciated seven ingredients
necessary in a leader in war, each of which is appropriate to the spiritual warfare: (1) He should be able
to sit back and avoid getting immersed in detail.
(2) He must not be petty. (3) He must not be pompous. (4) He must be a good picker of men. (5) He
should trust those under him and let them get on with
their job without interference. (6) He must have the
power of clear decision. (7) He should inspire confidence.[8]

Dr. John R. Mott moved in student circles, and his
tests covered different territory: (1) Does he do little
things well? (2) Has he learned the meaning of priorities? (3) How does he use his leisure? (4) Has
he intensity? (5) Has he learned to take advantage
of momentum? (6) Has he the power of growth?
(7) What is his attitude toward discouragements?
(8) How does he face impossible situations? (9)
What are his weakest points?[9]

Since leadership is essentially the power of one man to influence another, it is well to consider the almost limitless possibilities of a single life for good or ill. Both Scripture and experience affirm that no one can be neutral, either morally or spiritually. On lives that come within the range of our influence we leave an indelible impress, whether we are conscious of it or not. Dr. John Geddie, for example, went to Aneityum in 1848 and worked there for God for twenty-four years. On the tablet erected to his memory these words are inscribed:

> When he landed, in 1848, there were no Christians.
> When he left, in 1872, there were no heathen.

When the burning zeal of the apostolic church resulted in converts multiplying at an extraordinary rate, the Holy Spirit taught a striking lesson on the nature of spiritual leadership. The exigencies of the work made such heavy demands on the apostles that the creation of a lower echelon of leaders to care for the neglected poor and widows became necessary. Those must be carefully selected, so the apostles specified the type of man to be chosen: "Select from among you, brethren, seven men of good reputation, full of the Spirit and of wisdom, whom we may put in charge of this task" (Acts 6:3).

Is it without significance that the central requirement is that they be "full of the Spirit," even for what might be termed a secular service? They were to be men of *integrity,* of good reputation; of *sagacity,* full of wisdom; of *spirituality,* full of the Spirit. Spirituality is not easy to define, but its presence or absence can easily be discerned. It has been called the diffused fragrance that has been assimilated in the garden of the Lord. It is the power to change the atmosphere by one's presence, the unconscious influence that makes Christ and spiritual things real to others.

If that is the standard for those who occupy the lower offices of the church, what of those who aspire to the higher? Spiritual ends can be achieved only by spiritual men who employ spiritual methods. What a far-reaching change could be effected in our churches and Christian organizations if that priority were strictly observed! Secular men, be they ever so gifted and charming in person, have no place in the leadership of the church, even in temporal matters.

The essential ideas of true spiritual leadership are gathered up in these words of John R. Mott:

> I have in mind the use of the word leadership which our Lord doubtless had in mind when He said, "He who would be greatest among you shall be the servant of all"—leadership in the sense of rendering the maximum of service; leadership in the sense of the largest unselfishness; in the sense of unwearying and unceasing absorption in the greatest work of the world, the building up of the kingdom of our Lord Jesus Christ.[10]

NOTES

1. Bernard L. Montgomery, *Memoirs of Field-Marshall Montgomery* (Cleveland: World, 1958), p. 70.
2. Lettie B. Cowman, *Charles E. Cowman* (Los Angeles: Oriental Missionary Society, 1928), p. 251.
3. Montgomery, p. 70.
4. Phyllis Thompson, *D. E. Hoste* (London: China Inland Mission, n.d), p. 122.
5. A. W. Tozer, in *The Reaper*, February, 1962, p. 459.
6. Paul E. Sangster, *Doctor Sangster* (London: Epworth, 1962), p. 109.
7. James Burns, *Revivals, Their Laws and Leaders* (London: Hodder & Stoughton, 1909), p. 95.
8. Montgomery, p. 70.
9. B. Matthews, *John R. Mott* (London: S.C.M. Press, 1934), p. 346.
10. Ibid., p. 353.

5

CRITERIA OF LEADERSHIP POTENTIAL

Send out for yourself men . . . every one a leader among them.

NUMBERS 13:2

Our Lord's assessment of leadership potential tended to cut right across the popular opinion and custom of that day, as well as of our own. Who would have chosen for a task with worldwide implications, such an unprepossessing group of untrained and uninfluential men as the apostles?

Would we not have aimed to include in our leadership group a prominent statesman, a clever financier, an influential member of the priesthood, an athletic star, a popular socialite, and a university professor? Jesus chose none of those. All his disciples came from the humbler people; they were not from the influential class but were men who were unspoiled by the sophistication of their day.

He chose laymen, rather than men from the religious hierarchy. When J. Hudson Taylor did the same thing and formed his missionary team for China mainly of lay men and women, the religious world was shocked; but today that is a widely recognized though not always approved procedure.

He did not choose scholars or even farmers, perhaps because their occupations would render them less amenable to the revolutionary leadership He would give. Almost all his disciples came from Galilee, not Judea. Life in "Galilee of the nations" was much more cosmopolitan than in exclusive Jerusalem, and the minds of Galileans were much more open to new ideas.

He chose men with little formal education for His shock troops, but they soon displayed remarkable flair and proved to be an elite corps.

It would hardly be too much to say that no one but Jesus would have discerned in that diverse group of men the style of leadership that gradually emerged as a result of their training years under the Master Teacher's skillful hand. To their latent talents they added fervent devotion and fierce loyalty, albeit with some isolated instances of failure.

Because qualities of natural leadership are by no means unimportant in spiritual leadership, there is value in seeking to discover leadership potential both in oneself and in others. Most people have latent and undeveloped traits that, through lack of self-analysis and consequent lack of self-knowledge, may long remain undiscovered. An objective study of the following suggested standards of self-measurement could result in the discovery of such qualities where they exist, as well as the detection of incipient weaknesses that would unfit one for leadership.

• Have you ever broken yourself of a bad habit? To lead others, one must be master of oneself.

• Do you retain control of yourself when things go wrong? The leader who loses self-control in testing circumstances forfeits respect and loses influence. He must be calm in crisis and resilient in adversity and disappointment.

• Do you think independently? While using to the full the thought of others, the leader cannot afford to let others do his thinking or make his decisions for him.

• Can you handle criticism objectively and remain unmoved under it? Do you turn it to good account? The humble man can derive benefit from petty and even malicious criticism.

• Can you use disappointments creatively?

• Do you readily secure the cooperation and win the respect and confidence of others?

• Do you possess the ability to secure discipline without having to resort to a show of authority? True leadership is an internal quality of the spirit and requires no external show of force.

• Have you qualified for the beatitude pronounced on the peacemaker? It is much easier to *keep* the peace than to *make* peace where it has been shattered. An important function in leadership is conciliation— the ability to discover common ground between opposing viewpoints and then induce both parties to accept it.

• Are you entrusted with the handling of difficult and delicate situations?

• Can you induce people to do happily some legitimate thing that they would not normally wish to do?

• Can you accept opposition to your viewpoint or decision without considering it a personal affront and reacting accordingly? Leaders must expect opposition and should not be offended by it.

• Do you find it easy to make and keep friends? Your circle of loyal friends is an index of the quality and extent of your leadership.

• Are you unduly dependent on the praise or approval of others? Can you hold a steady course in the face of disapproval and even temporary loss of confidence?

• Are you at ease in the presence of your superiors or strangers?

• Do your subordinates appear at ease in your presence? A leader should give an impression of sympathetic understanding and friendliness that will put others at ease.

• Are you really interested in people? In people of all types and all races? Or do you entertain respect of persons? Is there hidden racial prejudice? An antisocial person is unlikely to make a good leader.

• Do you possess tact? Can you anticipate the likely effect of a statement before you make it?

• Do you possess a strong and steady will? A leader will not long retain his position if he is vacillating.

• Do you nurse resentments, or do you readily forgive injuries done to you?

• Are you reasonably optimistic? Pessimism is no asset to a leader.

• Are you in the grip of a master passion such as that of Paul, who said, "This *one thing* I do"? Such a singleness of motive will focus all one's energies and powers on the desired objective.

• Do you welcome responsibility?

R. E. Thompson suggests these tests of our attitudes to people as an indication of our capacity for leadership:

Do other people's failures annoy us or challenge us?

Do we use people or cultivate people?

Do we direct people or develop people?

Do we criticize or encourage?

Do we shun the problem person or seek him out?[1]

It will not be sufficient merely to engage in this exercise in self-analysis superficially and pay no further heed to the discoveries made. Something must be done about it. Why not take some of the points of conscious weakness and failure and, in cooperation with the Holy Spirit who is the Spirit of discipline, concentrate on strengthening or correcting them?

Those desirable qualities were all present in their fullness in the symmetrical character of our Lord, and each Christian should make it his constant prayer that they might more rapidly be incorporated into his own personality.

There are other qualities that detract from leadership ability, for example, an oversensitive and defensive attitude when checked or corrected. There is always some element of truth in such criticism, and self-vindication is an unproductive quality.

An unwillingness to accept responsibility for failure, or the tendency to lay the blame at someone else's door will forfeit confidence.

Inflexibility and intolerance in attitude is likely to alienate the worker who is creative and ambitious.

While always aiming at excellence, one should avoid the snare of perfectionism. The perfectionist usually sets goals quite beyond his ability to attain and then entertains a false sense of guilt because of failure to achieve. We live in an imperfect world, and we must come to terms with the possible. Setting more modest and realistic goals would bring great release to many an idealistic perfectionist.

Inability to keep a confidence has cost many a leader his influence with his people. Similarly the inability to yield a point, and thus shatter the image of infallibility, will achieve the same result.

NOTES

1. R. E. Thompson, in *World Vision,* December, 1966, p. 4.

6

PAULINE SIDELIGHTS ON LEADERSHIP

An overseer, then, must be above reproach, the husband of one wife, temperate, prudent, respectable, hospitable, able to teach, not addicted to wine or pugnacious, but gentle, uncontentious, free from the love of money. He must be one who manages his own household well, keeping his children under control with all dignity . . . and not a new convert, lest he become conceited. . . . And he must have a good reputation with those outside the church.

1 Timothy 3:2-7

A friend of the author once said to him, "Isn't it a humbling experience to see your own faults running around on two little legs!" Sometimes we can see spiritual principles more clearly when they are exemplified in personality than when they are stated in the abstract. In the apostle Paul himself we see exemplified the qualities he stated were essential to effective spiritual leadership.

It is characteristic of truly great leaders that their stature looms larger with the passing of the years. When viewed from any standpoint, Paul grows in moral and spiritual grandeur the more critically he is analyzed. It is small wonder that A. W. Tozer designated him the world's most successful Christian. How amazing that God should select the most ruthless and aggressive enemy of the church and transform him into its most outstanding leader and chief apologist!

He was uniquely equipped for the global role to which God called him. An anonymous writer suggested as a present-day parallel to Paul, one who could speak in Peking in Chinese, quoting Confucius and Mencius; write closely-reasoned theology in English and expound it in Oxford; and defend his cause before the Soviet Academy of Sciences in Russian in Moscow. He was certainly one of the most versatile leaders the church has known.

His versatility is seen in the ease with which he adapted himself to his audience. He appears equally at ease with statesmen and soldiers, women and children, kings and officials. He was perfectly at home in debate with philosophers, theologians, or idolators.

His religious training under Gamaliel, one of Jewry's seven most influential rabbis, gave him a great grasp of the Old Testament, and he proved a brilliant student. His own testimony was: "I was advancing in Judaism beyond many of my contemporaries among my countrymen, being more extremely zealous for my ancestral traditions" (Gal. 1:14).

A natural leader, when he became chained to his Master's chariot wheel, he developed into a great moral and spiritual leader, wielding great authority.

His boundless, Christ-centered ambition was kindled by the powerful motives of a supreme love for Christ and an inescapable sense of obligation (Rom. 1:14; 2 Cor. 5:14). He had the authentic missionary passion to share his great discovery—a passion that overrode all cultural differences and overleaped all racial barriers. He felt equally indebted to all men. Poverty or wealth, social status or intellectual attainment were equally irrelevant.

With such a background, who would be better qualified to catalog the requisites of spiritual leadership than Paul himself? In addition to the richness of his own experience, he enjoyed the illumination and inspiration of the Holy Spirit. Spiritual standards do not change from generation to generation, but remain the same in the space age as at the birth of the church. None of the qualities here enjoined by Paul are optional extras, but indispensable requirements.

It is generally held that the two words used of leaders in the church—*bishops* and *elders*—were applicable to the same person. *Elder* had reference to his dignity and status, whereas *bishop* related to his function or duty. In other words, one word had reference to his person, the other to his work. That is borne out by such passages as Acts 20:17 and 28, where Paul addresses the same people first as elders and then as bishops. The present connotation of *bishop* was a considerably later development.

The paragraph at the head of this chapter specifies the qualifications to be expected in a spiritual leader, in several spheres and relationships.

SOCIAL QUALIFICATIONS

In respect to those within the church, the leader is to be *above reproach*. His character is to be such as will not leave him open to attack or censure. Colloquially stated, detractors will not have "a rung to stand on." If a charge were preferred against him, it would fall to the ground because his life would afford no grounds for reproach. He must give no opening for his adversary even to launch a smear campaign.

As to those without the church, he is to be *of good reputation*. The person who associates with a Christian in daily secular life and work or in extrachurch activities often has the clearest insight into the genuineness of his Christian character. The reason for this requirement is obvious. An elder known to the author was a businessman who sometimes took preaching appointments on the Lord's Day. His employees used to say that they could always tell when he had been preaching on Sunday because he was unusually bad-tempered on Monday. He did not influence his employees toward Christ.

Despite their criticisms, non-Christians generally respect the high ideals of Christian character and, when they see them actually reproduced before them in a holy life, covet a similar experience. It is that very fact that lends point to their criticisms. The character of an elder should be such as commands the respect of the outsider, inspires his confidence, and arouses his aspiration. Example is much more potent than precept.

MORAL QUALIFICATIONS

In a world in which moral principles come under subtle and constant attack, a leader must be blameless in that respect. He is to be *"one wife's husband,"* in a society where that is far from being the norm. There are several interpretations of the phrase, but whatever else it means, it certainly indicates that he must be blameless in his moral life. He must set a high standard in the marital relationship in his faithfulness to a sole marriage partner. He must be a man of unchallengeable morality.

He must also be *temperate,* "not addicted to wine," with all that is involved in that statement. The word signifies "one who lingers by his wine," with the probable result of becoming drunk and disorderly. A drunken man is disgraced in ordinary society, and how much more in the Christian church? A leader must allow himself no indulgence in secret that would undermine his character or mar his public witness.

MENTAL QUALIFICATIONS

He should be *prudent,* sound-minded. This word indicates "the well-balanced state of mind resulting from habitual self-restraint" and refers to the inner character that results from daily self-discipline. Jeremy Taylor termed this quality "reason's girdle and passion's bridle."[1] The Greeks placed great value upon it. To them it was the state of mind that was disciplined, not swayed by sudden impulse, that did not fly to extremes but was the mean between them. For example, courage is the mean between rashness and timidity; purity is the mean between prudery and immorality. The leader who possesses a sound mind is in control of every part of his nature.

As to his outer conduct, he must be *respectable,* decorous. The word is *kosmos,* the order that emerged out of chaos at the fiat of God. A well-ordered life is the outcome of a well-ordered mind. The life of the leader should be so ordered as to reflect the beauty and orderliness of God.

Mentally and spiritually, he should be *able to teach*. The word implies not only ability but readiness to teach; a desire and constraint to impart to others the truth that the Holy Spirit has taught him from the Scriptures. If he is to teach, he himself must be a student of the Scriptures. "Any man who shows himself incapable of successfully teaching others is not qualified for the eldership," said H. A. Kent. The spiritual leader is responsible for teaching those under him to a greater or lesser degree, and his instruction must have the support of a blameless life.

Samuel Brengle lamented:

> Oh, for more teachers among us; leaders who know how to read hearts and apply truth to the

needs of the people, as a good physician reads his patients and applies remedies to their ills. There are soul-sicknesses open and obscure, acute and chronic, superficial and deep-seated which the truth as it is in Jesus will heal. But it is not the same truth for each need, any more than the same medicine for every disease. This is why we should most diligently study the Bible and pray for the constant and powerful illumination of the Spirit.[2]

John Wesley was a man who possessed those mental qualities to a high degree. He never indulged in a cheap disparagement of the intellect and was always seeking to raise the intellectual as well as the moral and spiritual condition of those around him. His own intellectual powers were of the highest order; had he chosen, he could have been in the front rank of the scholars of his day. He had a wonderful knowledge of literature. An eminent preacher declared that he knew of no sermons that evinced so intimate a knowledge of classical and general literature as those of Wesley. And yet he was known as a "man of one Book." He was a shining example of consecrated intellect.

PERSONALITY QUALIFICATIONS

The Christian leader must not be *pugnacious,* but genial and *gentle;* not a contentious controversialist, but one who is sweetly reasonable. Those contrasting words give an attractive angle to the character of the ideal leader. Of the word *gentle,* R. C. Trench says,

"It is the spirit which rectifies and redresses the injustices of justice." The person who possesses this quality, according to Aristotle, "remembers good rather than evil, the good one has received rather than the good one has done." He will be actively considerate and forbearing rather than merely uncontentious; irenic in disposition, always seeking a peaceful solution to a thorny problem or an explosive situation.

Then, too, he must be *hospitable,* a friend of strangers. That ministry will not be regarded as an irksome imposition, but instead as a privileged service done for his Lord. In the early book *The Shepherd of Hermas* it is stated that a bishop "must be hospitable, a man who gladly and at all times welcomes into his house the servants of God."

When Paul wrote, hospitality of that kind was much more essential than in our own times, although it is still a desirable grace in a leader—and in a leader's wife, for it is she who has to bear much of the load. In the days of the early church, inns were few, and those few were both dirty and immoral. Visiting Christians or teachers could not resort to the homes of the heathen. As persecution spread, upon entering another city Christians were liable to be hunted down and sold as slaves. It was therefore essential that church members, and especially leaders, should extend hospitality to them. There must be an open door for fellow Christians and non-Christians too.

A friend of the author who had large business responsibilities as well as heavy church commitments made it a practice to keep an open home for visitors or the unprivileged on the Lord's Day. Besides making a fine contribution to the life and atmosphere of the church, his own spiritual leadership was enhanced, his life enriched, and others blessed.

Covetousness and its twin, *love of money,* are disqualifying factors. In the exercise of his spiritual ministry, the leader must never be swayed by considerations of financial reward. He will be as willing to accept an appointment with a lower remuneration as one with a higher.

Fletcher of Madeley was described thus by Wesley: "As unblameable a character in every respect I have not found, either in Europe or America; and I scarce expect such another on this side of eternity." Previous to Fletcher's going to Madeley, with which his name is inseparably linked, it is told that his benefactor, Mr. Hill, informed him that he could have the position in Dunham in Cheshire, adding: "The parish is small, the duty is light, the income is good (£400 per annum), and it is situated in a fine healthy sporting country!"

"Alas, sir," replied Fletcher, "Dunham will not suit me. There is too much money and too little labor."

"Few clergymen make such objections," remarked Mr. Hill. "It is a pity to decline such a living, as I do not know that I can find you another. Would you like Madeley?"

"That, sir, would be the very place for me."

"My object is to make you comfortable in your own way," said Mr. Hill. "If you prefer Madeley, I shall find no difficulty in persuading the present vicar to exchange it for Dunham, which is worth more than twice as much."

In that small church that man who was innocent of covetousness and devoid of the love of money exercised a remarkable ministry, and through his biography his influence is still being felt in this generation.

DOMESTIC QUALIFICATIONS

The Christian leader who is married must demonstrate his ability to rule his home in a godly way—"one who manages his own household well, keeping his children under control with all dignity." Is it not failure in this realm that has caused many ministers and missionaries to fall short of the highest in their leadershp? "Dignity" is a better rendering than ' gravity" in the King James Version, because it avoids the picture of unsmiling sternness while still retaining the idea of due respect.

To attain this ideal, a man must have a wife who fully shares his spiritual aspirations and is willing to make the necessary sacrifices. Many a gifted man has been lost to high office and spiritual effectiveness because of the unsuitability of the wife he has chosen. If a man has not succeeded in exercising a benevolent and happy discipline in his own family, is there reason to expect that he will do better with the family of God? If his home is not well ordered nor his children well controlled, his ability to offer worthy hospitality will be greatly restricted, and his influence on other families diminished.

The clear implication is that, while caring for the

interests of the church or other spiritual activity, the leader will not neglect the family, which is his personal and primary responsibility. In the economy of God, the discharge of one God-given duty or responsibility will never involve the neglect of another. There is time for the full discharge of every legitimate duty. Paul implies that the ability of a man to exercise spiritual authority over others is evidenced by his ability to exercise a wise and loving discipline in his own home. Leadership has often been forfeited through failure in that realm.

MATURITY QUALIFICATIONS

Spiritual maturity is indispensable to good leadership. There is no place for a novice, a new convert, in positions of responsibility. The word is our *neophyte* and means "newly planted," a figure taken from nature. A plant needs time to take root and come to maturity, and the process cannot be hurried. It must take root downward before it can bear fruit upward. In harmony with that figure, Bengel said that novices usually have "an abundance of verdure. The convert is not yet pruned by the cross." In 1 Timothy 3:10, referring to the qualifications of a deacon, Paul urges, "Let these also first be tested." That will prove their worthiness or otherwise for a position of responsibility in the church.

When Timothy became pastor of the church at Ephesus, it had already been in existence for more than a decade. It had enjoyed a galaxy of gifted pastors and teachers, so there were many men of mature experience in it; hence Paul's insistence on the necessity of that quality in its leaders. In the light of missionary experience in the guidance of emerging churches, it is interesting to note that Paul, always realistic, does not demand that qualification in the case of the recently established Cretan church, for there were no such men available (Titus 1:5-9). The ideal cannot be insisted on in the early stages of church-building; but every care should be taken in the selection of those asked to assume responsibility to ensure that they are stable in character, spiritual in outlook, and not ambitious for position.

Paul advances a valid and convincing reason for the requirement: "Lest being lifted up with pride, he fall into the condemnation of the devil." A recent convert lacks the spiritual maturity and stability essential to wise leadership. It is unwise to give key positions too early even to those who manifest promising talent, lest it spoil them. The history of the church and missions is strewn with tragic illustrations of that possibility. Such an appointment would be in the best interests of neither the new convert nor the church. Human nature being what it is, the novice would stand in great danger of being inflated with a sense of his own importance by too sudden an elevation to a place of authority over his fellows. But although he should not be given a key position too soon, the promising convert should be afforded a widening opportunity to serve at humbler and less prominent tasks that would develop both natural and spiritual gifts. He should not be advanced too fast, lest he be-

come puffed up. Neither should he be repressed, lest
he be discouraged.

In harmony with that ruling, as William Hendriksen
points out, Paul did not appoint elders in every place
on his first missionary journey, but only after he had
revisited the churches and satisfied himself of the
spiritual progress of those whom he then appointed
(Acts 14:23). Nor was Timothy ordained immediately on his conversion. Although his conversion
took place on Paul's first journey, he was not ordained
until the second journey at the earliest.[3]

"It is the mark of a grown-up man, as compared
with a callow youth, that he finds his centre of gravity wherever he happens to be at the moment, and
however much he longs for the object of his desire,
it cannot prevent him from staying at his post and
doing his duty," wrote Dietrich Bonhoeffer. That is
just what a new convert finds difficult to do. It is a
characteristic that accompanies a growing maturity.

Maturity is exhibited in magnanimity of spirit and
breadth of outlook. Paul's encounter with Christ
transformed him from a narrow-minded bigot into the
most magnanimous of men. The indwelling of Christ
enlarged his heart and broadened his horizons. Yet
his breadth of outlook did not lead him to abandon
his convictions.

The above requirements for leadership in the Christian church are recognized as essential even in worldly circles. William Barclay quotes a pagan, Onosander
by name, who gave this description of the ideal commander: "He must be prudently self-controlled, sober,

frugal, enduring in toil, intelligent, without love of money, neither young nor old, if possible the father of a family, able to speak competently, and of good reputation."[4] The similarity to Paul's list is striking. If the world demands such standards of its leaders, is it too much to expect all those and more of leaders in the church of God?

NOTES

1. William Barclay, *Letters to Timothy and Titus* (Edinburgh: St. Andrews, 1960), p. 92.
2. C. W. Hall, *Samuel Logan Brengle* (New York: Salvation Army, 1933), p. 112.
3. W. Hendriksen, *1 and 2 Timothy and Titus* (London: Banner of Truth, 1959), p. 36.
4. Barclay, p. 86.

7

PETRINE SIDELIGHTS ON LEADERSHIP

Therefore, I exhort the elders among you, as your fellow elder and witness of the sufferings of Christ, and a partaker also of the glory that is to be revealed, shepherd the flock of God among you, exercising oversight, not under compulsion, but voluntarily, according to the will of God; and not for sordid gain, but with eagerness, nor yet as lording it over those allotted to your charge, but proving to be examples to the flock. And when the Chief Shepherd appears, you will receive the unfading crown of glory. You younger men, likewise, be subject to your elders; and all of you, clothe yourselves with humility toward one another, for "God is opposed to the proud, but gives grace to the humble." Humble yourselves, therefore, under the mighty hand of God, that He may exalt you at the proper time, casting all your anxiety upon Him, because He cares for you.

1 PETER 5:1-7

Peter was the natural and accepted leader of the apostolic band. What Peter did, the others did. Where Peter went, the others went. "I go afishing," said Peter. "We also go with thee," rejoined his friends. His mistakes, which sprang mostly from his incurable impetuosity, were many; but his influence was great and his leadership unchallenged. To ponder his advice, written to spiritual leaders in the years of his maturity, is a valuable exercise. He wrote to the guides of a persecuted church some of the timeless principles that relate to every type of spiritual leadership.

The veteran shepherd reminded them of their primary responsibility to the flock committed to their care: See that your "flock of God" is properly fed and cared for (5:2). Undertones of his never-to-be-forgotten private interview with the Chief Shepherd after his tragic failure are not difficult to detect (John 21:15-17). Indeed, in this passage he seems to be living again the experiences of those early days. He well knew that those who were passing through deep trial, as were "the strangers of the dispersion" (1:1) to whom he was writing, needed the highest type of pastoral care. With that in view he wrote to the elders.

It should be noted that Peter did not write as chief of the apostles, but as a "fellow-elder," one who was bearing similar responsibilities. He spoke to them not from above, but from alongside—a good vantage ground for the exercise of leadership. He treated them as being on an equality with himself. He wrote, too, as a witness of the sufferings of Christ, one whose heart had been chastened by his own failure, broken and conquered by Calvary's love. A shepherd's work cannot be done effectively without a shepherd's heart.

First, Peter dealt with the leader's *motivation*. The spiritual leader is to assume and discharge his responsibility uncoerced, not under compulsion, but "willingly and not because you feel you can't get out of it." Conditions prevailing at the time Peter wrote were such as could have daunted the stoutest heart, but he urged the leaders not to hold back on that account. Nor were they to serve merely out of a sense of duty or through the pressure of circumstances but under the loftier constraint of divine love.

The pastoral ministry was to be exercised "according to . . . God" (5:2), not according to their own preferences and desires.

> Peter says to the leaders, "Shepherd your people *like God*." Just as Israel is God's special allotment, the people we have to serve in the church or anywhere else are our special allotment; and our whole attitude to them must be the attitude of God; we must shepherd them like God. What a vision opens out! What an ideal! And what a condemnation! It is our task to show people the forbearance of God, the forgiveness of God, the seeking love of God, the illimitable service of God.[1]

Service to which God calls must not be refused because of a sense of unworthiness or inadequacy. Whoever could be worthy of such a trust? And as for inadequacy, it should be remembered that Moses' plea for exemption on that ground, far from pleasing God, kindled His anger (Exod. 4:14).

The spiritual leader must be *disinterested in gain* in his service. Do your work not for what you can make out of it, "not for shameful gain" (RSV*). Peter had not forgotten the corrupting power of covetousness on his companion Judas, and he was concerned that his fellow elders should be entirely free from avarice. The leader is not to be affected in his service or decisions by any considerations of financial or other gain. When people see he is genuinely disinterested, his words will carry greater weight.

Dr. Paul Rees suggests that greed for money is not the only thought contained in the Greek words "shameful gain."[2] The phrase might as appropriately be applied to greed for popularity or fame, an equally insidious temptation. Prestige and power are often coveted more than money.

"I am not sure which of the two occupies the lower sphere, he who hungers for money or he who thirsts for applause," wrote Dr. J. H. Jowett. "A preacher may dress and smooth his message to court the public cheers, and labourers in other spheres may bid for prominence, for imposing print, for grateful recognition. All this unfits us for our task. It destroys his perception of the needs and perils of the sheep."[3]

The Christian leader must not be *dictatorial*. "Nor yet as lording it over those allotted to your charge" (5:3*a*). An ambitious leader can easily degenerate

Revised Standard Version.

into a petty tyrant with a domineering manner. "Even
a little authority is prone to turn the seemly walk into
the offensive strut." No attitude could be less becoming for one who professes to be a servant of the Son
of God, who humbled Himself.

He must set *a worthy example* for his flock. "Proving to be examples to the flock" (5:3b)—words rem-
iniscent of Paul's exhortation to Timothy: "In speech,
conduct, love, faith, and purity, show yourself an example of those who believe" (1 Tim. 4:12). Peter
reminds the elders of the spirit in which their ministry
was to be exercised—the shepherd spirit. The word
feed implies the complete task of the shepherd. Lest
they should assume prerogatives not rightly theirs, he
reminds them that it is God's flock, not theirs, and it
is to Him they are finally accountable. He is the chief
Shepherd, they are His undershepherds.

If it is "according to God," the shepherding ministry will surely include intercession. The saintly
Bishop Azariah of India once remarked to Bishop
Stephen Neill that he found time every day to pray by
name for everyone in a position of leadership in his
extensive diocese. Small wonder that during his thirty
years of office the diocese trebled in its membership
and greatly increased in spiritual effectiveness.[4]

The leader is to be "clothed with humility." The
word "clothed" occurs only here and refers to the
white garment, or apron, worn by a slave. The leader
is to *don the slave's apron*. Was Peter recalling the
tragic night when he refused to take the towel and gird

himself and wash his Master's feet? He must guard them against a similar tragedy. Pride ever lurks at the heels of power, but God will not encourage proud men in His service. Rather will He oppose and obstruct them. But to the undershepherd who is humble and lowly in heart, He will multiply grace. In verse 5, Peter exhorted that the leader *act humbly* in his relations with others. But in verse 6 he challenged him to *react humbly* to the disciplines of God. "Therefore humbly submit to God's strong hand" is Charles B. Williams' rendering, bringing out the significance of the passive voice of the verb. "Allow yourselves to be humbled" conveys the correct idea.

As an inducement to the highest type of leadership, Peter held out another powerful incentive: "When the Chief Shepherd appears, you will receive the unfading crown of glory" (5:4). "Unfading" here means "unwithering." The coveted wreath of laurel or parsley would soon fade or wither, but not the garland of amaranth, the reward of the faithful leader.

The undershepherd may also derive comfort from the fact that he will not be left by the Chief Shepherd to shoulder his burdens alone. He can experience a transference of anxiety. "Cast all your cares on Him, for you are His charge" (5:7, NEB). And it is the cares incidental to leadership of which Peter was speaking. *Anxiety* implies "distraction of mind and heart in view of conflicting emotions." But the undershepherd need have no fear that the cares of his flock of God will be too heavy for him. By a definite act of mind and will, he can transfer the crushing weight of his spiritual burdens to the powerful shoulders of the God who cares.

NOTES

1. William Barclay, *The Letters of Peter and Jude* (Edinburgh: St. Andrews, 1958), p. 156.
2. Paul S. Rees, *Triumphant in Trouble* (London: Marshall, Morgan & Scott, n.d.), p. 126.
3. J. H. Jowett, *The Epistles of Peter* (London: Hodder & Stoughton, n.d.), p. 188.
4. Stephen Neill, *On the Ministry* (n.p., n.d.), pp. 107-8.

8

QUALITIES ESSENTIAL TO LEADERSHIP—1

An overseer, then, must be above reproach, the husband of one wife, temperate, prudent, respectable, hospitable, able to teach, not addicted to wine or pugnacious, but gentle, uncontentious, free from the love of money. He must be one who manages his own household well, keeping his children under control with all dignity (but if a man does not know how to manage his own household, how will he take care of the church of God?); and not a new convert, lest he become conceited and fall into the condemnation incurred by the devil. And he must have a good reputation with those outside the church, so that he may not fall into reproach and the snare of the devil.

1 TIMOTHY 3:2-7

When Jesus was preparing His disciples for their future role, He displayed a superb training method.

He taught them by example as well as by precept, and His teaching was incidental rather than formal. He arranged retreats for special instruction, but in the main their characters were developed in the highways of life rather than in isolation. Their experiences in daily life afforded the opportunity of inculcating spiritual principles and values. He employed the internship method (e.g., Luke 10:17-24) and that enabled them to learn by their failures as well as their successes (Mark 9:14-29). They learned to exercise faith for their daily needs. He delegated authority and responsibility to them as they were able to bear it. The wonderful discourse of John 13-16 has been termed their graduation address. We could not do better than follow the example of the supreme Teacher and Exemplar of spiritual leadership.

In preparing a man for leadership, God always has in view the sphere of service to which He purposes to call him. He is able therefore to adapt the means to the end and endow him with gifts of nature and grace that will best fit him to fulfill his commission. Without the superb equipment and unique training that were granted to him, Paul would never have achieved the incredible results he did within the space of one short life.

God prepared Adoniram Judson to pioneer His work in Burma by endowing him with the appropriate qualities—self-reliance balanced by humility, energy restrained by prudence, patience, self-forgetfulness, courage, and a passion for souls.

Martin Luther, the great Reformer, was described

as a man easy of approach; totally without personal vanity; so simple in his tastes that men wondered how he could sustain life on so little; abounding in solid sense, playful humor, and mirthfulness; honest as the day, transparently sincere. Added to that was his undaunted courage, inflexible conviction, and passion for Christ. It is small wonder that he bound men to him with bonds of steel.[1]

Professor G. Warneck described Hudson Taylor in terms that indicated how appropriately God had endowed him for his work of pioneering in China: "A man full of faith and the Holy Ghost, of entire surrender to God and His call, of great self-denial, heartfelt compassion, rare power in prayer, marvellous organizing faculty, indefatigable perseverance, and of astounding influence with men, and withal of childlike simplicity himself."

In each case those men were endowed with gifts that uniquely equipped them for the special tasks to which they were later called. But that which raised them above their fellows was the degree to which they developed those gifts and graces through devotion and self-discipline.

We shall consider the general qualities that go to make a man a spiritual leader and that require to be continually developed by the possessor.

DISCIPLINE

It has been well said that the future is with the disciplined, and that quality has been placed first in our list, for without it the other gifts, however great, will never realize their maximum potential. Only the disciplined person will rise to his highest powers. He is able to lead because he has conquered himself.

The words *disciple* and *discipline* are derived from the same root. A leader is a person who has first submitted willingly and learned to obey a discipline imposed from without, but who then imposes on himself a much more rigorous discipline from within. Those who rebel against authority and scorn self-discipline seldom qualify for leadership of a high order. They shirk the rigors and sacrifices it demands and reject the divine disciplines that are involved. Many who drop out of missionary work do so not because they are not sufficiently gifted but because there are large areas of their lives that have never been brought under the control of the Holy Spirit. The lazy and disorganized never rise to true leadership.

Many who take courses in leadership in the hope of attaining it fail because they have never learned to follow. They are like the boys who were playing war in the street. When a passerby inquired why they were so quiet and were doing nothing, one lad replied, "We are all generals. We can't get anyone to do the fighting."

Dr. Donald Barnhouse drew attention to the striking fact that the average age of the forty thousand biographies in the American *Who's Who*—the forty thousand who really run America—was just under twenty-eight. That throws into relief the important fact that the discipline in early life, which is prepared to make sacrifices in order to gain adequate preparation for the life-task, paves the way for high achievement.

A great statesman made a speech that turned the tide in national affairs. "May I ask how long it took you to prepare that speech?" asked an admirer.

"All my life has been a preparation for what I said today," he replied.

The young man of leadership caliber will work while others waste time, study while others sleep, pray while others play. There will be no place for loose or slovenly habits in word or thought, deed or dress. He will observe a soldierly discipline in diet and deportment, so that he might wage a good warfare. He will without reluctance undertake the unpleasant task that others avoid or the hidden duty that others evade because it evokes no applause or wins no appreciation. A Spirit-filled leader will not shrink from facing up to difficult situations or persons, or from grasping the nettle when that is necessary. He will kindly and courageously administer rebuke when that is called for; or he will exercise necessary discipline when the interests of the Lord's work demand it. He will not procrastinate in writing the difficult letter. His letter-basket will not conceal the evidences of his failure to grapple with urgent problems. His prayer will be:

> God, harden me against myself,
>> The coward with pathetic voice
>> Who craves for ease and rest and joy.
> Myself, arch-traitor to myself,
>> My hollowest friend,

My deadliest foe,
My clog, whatever road I go.

AMY WILSON CARMICHAEL*

Few men were more faithful and courageous in loving rebuke or in speaking frankly to people, when they or the work of God required it, than Fred Mitchell, who was British director of the China Inland Mission and chairman of the English Keswick Convention. Though unusually sensitive and affectionate in nature, he did not shirk the unpleasant interview. When he had something of that nature to say, it was always done in prayerfulness and with love, but not everyone was able to accept the admonition in the same spirit. He confided that he had suffered greatly when in a few cases his faithfulness had resulted in the estrangement of a friend.

As he drew toward the close of his life, it was observed by a friend that "he changed considerably. Although he did not avoid performing an unpleasant task when necessary, he would spend more time in prayer beforehand." Often when he had to deal with a matter of discipline or cut across the desires of others, he would write a letter and then keep it for several days. Sometimes on rereading it, he was assured it was right to send it, and it would be mailed. Sometimes it would be destroyed and another one written.[2]

When Dr. Thomas Cochrane, founder of the World Dominion Movement, was being interviewed for the mission field, he was asked, "To what position of the

*Used by permission of Christian Literature Crusade, Fort Washington, Pa.

field do you feel yourself specially called?" He answered, "I only know I should wish it to be the hardest you could offer me"—the reply of a strongly disciplined man.

Lytton Strachey wrote of Florence Nightingale:

> It was not by gentle sweetness and womanly self-abnegation that she brought order out of chaos in the Scutari Hospitals, that from her own resources she had clothed the British Army, that she had spread her dominion over the serried and reluctant powers of the official world; it was by strict method, by *stern discipline*, by rigid attention to detail, by ceaseless labour, by the fixed determination of an indomitable will. Beneath her cool and calm demeanour, there lurked fierce and passionate fires.

Samuel Chadwick, the great Methodist preacher and principal of Cliff College, made a great impact on his generation. He disciplined himself with rigor, rising at six in the morning and having a cold bath, summer and winter. He accustomed himself to do with little sleep. His study light was seldom extinguished before two in the morning. That rigorous program was but the outward expression of his inner discipline.[3]

All through his life, George Whitefield was an early riser; his usual hour for rising throughout the year was four o'clock. He was equally punctual in retiring at night. As the clock struck ten, no matter who were his visitors or what conversation was going on at the moment, he rose from his seat and, advancing toward the door, he would say good-naturedly to his friends, "Come, gentlemen, it is time for all good folks to be at home."[4]

> Barclay Buxton of Japan used to urge Christians to lead disciplined lives whether they were in business or evangelistic work. This included discipline in Bible study and prayer, in tithing their money, in use of their time, in keeping healthy by proper food and sleep and exercise. It included the rigor of disciplined fellowship among Christians who differed from each other in many ways. This discipline was to equip them to carry responsibility. He then urged them to take their place on committees and to fulfil their responsibility by careful thought, work and judgment. All these were the disciplines of his life, and his urgings for others came because of experience.[5]

These pieces of biography serve only to illustrate the fact that:

> The heights by great men reached and kept
> Were not attained by sudden flight;
> But they, while their companions slept,
> Were toiling upward in the night.
>
> AUTHOR UNKNOWN

Because the leader is himself so strongly disciplined, others sense that and are usually willing to respond cooperatively to the discipline he expects of them.

There is another little-emphasized element in discipline that merits attention. It is the discipline of being willing to receive from others as well as to give to others. There are some who delight in sacrificing themselves for others, who are quite unwilling to allow others to reciprocate. They are unwilling to place themselves under obligation to others. Yet that is a very powerful way of exercising helpful leadership. To neglect it is to rob both oneself and others.

It is told of Bishop Westcott that at the end of his life he said that he had made one great mistake, for, although he had always been willing to do for others to the limit of his ability, he had never been willing to let others do for him, and as a result some element of sweetness and completeness was missing. He had not allowed himself the discipline of receiving many kindnesses that could not be repaid.

VISION

Those who have most powerfully and permanently influenced their generation have been the "seers"— men who have seen more and farther than others— men of faith, for faith is vision. That was true of the prophets, or seers, of the Old Testament times. Moses, one of the greatest leaders of all time, "endured as seeing him who is invisible." His faith imparted vision. Elijah's servant saw with great vividness the vastness of the encircling army. Elijah saw the invincible environing host of heaven who were invisible to his servant. His faith imparted vision.

Powhattan James in his biography of George W. Truett, the great Baptist leader, wrote:

The man of God must have *insight* into things
spiritual. He must be able to see the mountains
filled with the horses and chariots of fire; he
must be able to interpret that which is written by
the finger of God upon the walls of conscience;
he must be able to translate the signs of the times
into terms of their spiritual meaning; he must be
able to draw aside, now and then, the curtain of
things material and let mortals glimpse the spiritual glories which crown the mercy seat of God.
The man of God must declare the pattern that
was shown him on the mount; he must utter the
vision granted to him upon the isle of revela-
tion. . . . None of these things can he do without
spiritual insight.[6]

That was a characteristic of Charles Cowman,
founder of the Oriental Missionary Society. "He was
a man of vision. Throughout his life he seemed to see
what the crowd did not see, and to see wider and
fuller than many of his own day. He was a man of
far horizons."[7]

Vision includes *foresight* as well as insight. It was
said of President McKinley that he was a great statesman because he had the faculty of putting his ear to
the ground and listening for things that were coming.
It is a different figure of speech, but it conveys the
same idea. He turned his listening into vision. He saw
what lay ahead. A leader must be able to envision the
end result of the policies or methods he advocates.
Responsible leadership always looks ahead to see how
policies proposed will affect not only present but succeeding generations.

The great missionary pioneers were without exception men of vision. Carey was seeing the whole world on the map while his fellow preachers were preoccupied with their own little parishes. Henry Martyn saw India, Persia, and Arabia—a vision of the Muslim world—while the church at home was engrossed in its petty theological squabbles. Of A. B. Simpson his contemporaries said, "His life-work seemed to be to push on alone, where his fellows had seen nothing to explore."

Speaking to Douglas Thornton of Egypt, Mr. Baylis, his senior missionary, remarked: "Thornton, you are different to anyone else I know. You are always looking at the end of things. Most people, myself included, find it better to do the next thing." Thornton's answer was: "I find that the constant inspiration gained by looking at the goal is the chief thing that helps me to persevere."[8] An ideal, a vision, was absolutely necessary to him. He could not work without it. And that explained the largeness of his views and the magnitude of his schemes.

Concerning Thornton's contribution to the Student Volunteer Movement, it was said: "He was the greatest prophet the Student Movement has ever had. He looked into the future and then devised his schemes." It was typical of his outlook to write to the leaders of his society: "I have been to the American Press at Beirut and seen there the result of the seven Arabian scholars after lifelong study, and I tell you it is as a drop in the ocean. We need a hymnology in Arabic, a whole range of topical theological works, an army of controversial tracts."[9]

Eyes that look are common. Eyes that see are rare. The Pharisees *looked* at Peter and saw only a poor unlettered fisherman, totally insignificant, not worthy of a second look. Jesus *saw* Peter and discovered the prophet and preacher, saint and leader of the unique band of men who turned the world upside down.

Vision includes *optimism and hope*. No pessimist ever made a great leader. The pessimist sees a difficulty in every opportunity. The optimist sees an opportunity in every difficulty. The pessimist, always seeing difficulties before possibilities, tends to hold back the man of vision who desires to push ahead. The cautious man has his part to play in helping his optimistic leader to be realistic as well. But he must watch lest his native and now ingrained caution clips the wings of the man God intends to soar. The cautious man draws valuable lessons from history and tradition, but he is in danger of being chained to the past. The man who sees the difficulties so clearly that he does not discern the possibilities will be unable to impart inspiration to his followers.

Browning described the courageous optimist:

> One who has never turned his back,
> But marched breast-forward,
> Never doubting clouds would break,
> Never dreamed, though right were worsted,
> Wrong would triumph.

Vision imparts venturesomeness, and history is on the side of venturesome faith. The man of vision is willing to take fresh steps of faith when there is only a seeming void beneath. The true leader does not play safe, but is willing to take calculated risks. Of Archbishop Mowll of Sydney it was said:

> It was a mark of his greatness that he was never behind his age, or too far ahead. He was up at the front, and far enough in advance to lead the march. He was always catching sight of new horizons. He still had a receptive mind for new ideas at an age when many were inclined to let things take their course.[10]

Although we should value the past and seek to profit by it, we should not consider it so sacred that we sacrifice the future for it. The man of vision looks to the future in his determination of current policy.

> Only vision makes a visionary.
> Only wisdom make a wiseacre.
> The combination of both is irresistible.

> A vision without a task makes a visionary.
> A task without a vision is drudgery.
> A vision with a task makes a missionary.[11]

WISDOM

"Wisdom is the faculty of making the use of knowledge, a combination of discernment, judgment, sagacity and similar powers. . . . In Scripture, right judgment concerning spiritual and moral truth" (Webster).

Wisdom is more than knowledge, which is the accumulation of facts. It has a personal connotation and implies sagacity. It is more than human acumen; it is heavenly discernment. It is knowledge with insight into the heart of things—that knows them as they really are. It involves the knowledge of God and of the intricacies of the human heart. It is much more than knowledge; it is the right application of knowledge in moral and spiritual matters, in meeting baffling situations, and in the complexity of human relationships. "Wisdom is nine-tenths a matter of being wise in time," said Theodore Roosevelt.[12] Most of us are "too often wise after the event."

Wisdom imparts necessary balance to a leader and delivers him from eccentricity and extravagance. Knowledge is gained by study, but when the Spirit fills a man, He imparts the wisdom to use and apply that knowledge correctly. "Full of wisdom" was one of the requirements for even subordinate leaders in the early church (Acts 6:3).

> Knowledge and wisdom, far from being one,
> Have ofttimes no connection. Knowledge dwells
> In heads replete with thoughts of other men:
> Wisdom, in minds attentive to their own.
> Knowledge is proud that he has learned so much,
> Wisdom is humble, that he knows no more.
>
> AUTHOR UNKNOWN

The place of wisdom in leadership was indicated in the statement of D. E. Hoste:

> When a man, in virtue of an official position demands obedience of another, irrespective of the latter's reason and conscience, this is the spirit of tyranny. When, on the other hand, by the exercise of tact and sympathy; by prayer, spiritual power and sound wisdom one is able to influence and enlighten another, so that he through the medium of his own reason and conscience is led to alter one course and adopt another, that is true spiritual leadership.[13]

Paul's prayer for the Christians at Colossae should constantly be on the lips of those bearing spiritual responsibility: "That you may be filled with the knowledge of His will *in all spiritual wisdom* and understanding" (Col. 1:9, italics added).

DECISION

When all the facts are in, swift and clear decision is the mark of the true leader. The man who possesses vision must do something about it, or he will remain a visionary, not a leader. Although he will be quick to reach a decision, that decision must be based on sound premises. Lord Montgomery includes the power of clear decision in his seven ingredients of military leadership.

Once a spiritual leader is sure of the will of God, he will go into immediate action, regardless of consequences. In pursuing his goal, he will have the courage to burn his bridges behind him. He must be willing to accept full responsibility for consequent failure or success and not place on a subordinate any blame that might accrue.

Abraham showed himself a man of swift and clear decision when faced with the crisis of the capture of Sodom and his nephew Lot. In his relations with Lot, Abraham manifested both active and passive sides of spirituality. In his unselfish yielding of his right to the choice of pasturelands, Abraham had displayed the passive graces of godliness. But when faced with that crisis, he displayed immediate decision and initiative. With great bravery he pursued the enemy with his pitifully inferior band of armed servants and, inspired by his faith in God, gained a resounding victory over his enemies.

Moses qualified to become the leader of Israel only when, after counting the cost, he made the momentous decision to abandon the treasures and pleasures of Egypt and identify himself with Israel in their sufferings and afflictions. It was his faith that nerved him to make such a far-reaching decision (Heb. 11:24-27).

It is significant that Paul's first question after his conversion was a key one and reflected this quality: "What shall I do, Lord?" (Acts 22:10). The moment he was convinced of the deity of Christ, he made the decision to yield Him unquestioning obedience. To be granted light was to follow it. To see his duty was to do it.

Each of the worthies immortalized in Hebrews 11 was a man of vision and decision. First they all saw the vision. Then they counted the cost, made their decisions, and acted on them. The same is true of the great missionary leaders. Carey saw the vision in Kettering and made his decision in the light of it, although the difficulties in realizing his vision loomed up to heaven. He gave effect to his vision in India. David Livingstone saw the vision in Dumbarton, made his decision, overcame all obstacles, and proceeded to bring it to fulfillment in Africa. Circumstances cannot frustrate such men, or difficulties deter them.

The true leader will resist the temptation to procrastinate in reaching a decision, nor will he vacillate after it has been made. Procrastination and vacillation are fatal to leadership. A sincere though faulty decision is better than no decision. Indeed the latter is really a decision, and often a wrong one. It is a decision that the status quo is acceptable. In most decisions the root problem is not so much in knowing what to do as in being prepared to live with the consequences.

It was said of Charles Cowman that he was a man of one purpose. He kept his eyes fixed on one great object. With him, a vision of possibility became action. The moment he found it possible to do a thing, he was uneasy until it was in course of execution.

A young man who was beginning his work with the Coast Guard was called early to take part in a desperate assignment. A great storm had arisen and a ship was signaling its distress. As the men began to move the big boat to the rescue, the young man, frightened at the fierceness of the gale, cried out to the captain, "We will never get back!" Above the storm the captain replied, "We don't have to come back, but we do have to go out."

COURAGE

Courage of the highest order is demanded of a spiritual leader—always moral courage and frequently physical courage as well. Courage is "that quality of mind which enables men to encounter danger or difficulty with firmness, or without fear or depression of spirits."

Paul was courageous both physically and morally, but his was not a courage that knew no fear. "I was with you in weakness and in fear and in much trembling" (1 Cor. 2:3). "For even when we came into Macedonia our flesh had no rest, but we were afflicted on every side: conflicts without, fears within" (2 Cor. 7:5). While not courting danger, he did not evade it if His Master's interests were at stake.

Martin Luther possessed this important quality in unusual measure. It has been asserted that he was perhaps as fearless a man as ever lived.[14] When he set out on his momentous journey to Worms he said, "You can expect from me everything save fear or recantation. I shall not flee, much less recant." His friends, warning him of the grave dangers he faced, sought to dissuade him. But Luther would not be dissuaded. "Not go to Worms!" he said. "I shall go to Worms though there were as many devils as tiles on the roofs."[15]

When Luther appeared before the emperor, he was called on to recant. They insisted that he should say in a word whether he would recant or no. "Unless convinced by the Holy Scripture, or by clear reasons from other sources, I cannot recant," he declared. "To Councils or Pope I cannot defer, for they have often erred. My conscience is a prisoner to God's Word."

When again given an opportunity to recant, he folded his hands: "Here I stand; I can do no other. God help me." A few days before his death, recalling that incident, Luther described his feelings: "I was afraid of nothing; God can make one so desperately bold. I know not whether I could be so cheerful now."

But not all are courageous by nature as Luther was, and that fact is both explicit and implicit in Scripture. The highest degree of courage is seen in the person who is most fearful but refuses to capitulate to it. However fearful they might have been, God's leaders in succeeding generations have been commanded to be of good courage. Had they been without fear, the command would have been pointless. The responsibility for his own courage is placed on the leader himself, for, since he is indwelt by the Spirit of power, there is possible attainment.

Contrast these two records: "The doors were shut where the disciples were [assembled], for fear of the Jews" (John 20:19) and, "They observed the confidence of Peter and John" (Acts 4:13). Those were the same disciples confronted by the same Jews after an interval of only a short time. Whence the new courage? Inspiration gives the answer: "They were all filled with the Holy Spirit." And when the Holy Spirit is ceded control of the whole personality, He imparts "not . . . a spirit of timidity, but of power" (2 Tim. 1:7).

The courage of a leader is demonstrated in his being willing to face unpleasant and even devastating facts and conditions with equanimity, and then acting with firmness in the light of them, even though it means incurring personal unpopularity. Human inertia and opposition do not deter him. His courage is not a thing of the moment but continues until the task is fully done.

People expect of their leaders courage and calmness in crisis. Others may falter and lose their heads, but not they. They strengthen their followers in the midst of shattering reverses and weakening influences.

Faced with Sennacherib's ruthless hordes, Hezekiah calmly made his military preparations and then set about strengthening the morale of his people. " 'Be strong and courageous,' " he exhorted them. " 'Do not fear or be dismayed because of the king of Assyria, nor because of all the multitude which is with him. . . . With him is only an arm[y] of flesh, but with us is the LORD our God to help us and to fight our battles.' *And the people* relied on the words of Hezekiah" (2 Chron. 32:7-8, italics added). That was leadershp indeed.

HUMILITY

Humility is the hallmark of the man whom God can use, although it is not in the world's curriculum. In the realm of politics and commerce, humility is a quality neither coveted nor required. There the leader needs and seeks prominence and publicity. But in God's scale of values, humility stands very high. Self-effacement, not self-advertisement, was Christ's definition of leadership. In training His disciples for their coming positions of authority, He told them they must not be pompous and overbearing like the Oriental despots, but humble and lowly like their Master (Matt. 20:25-27). The spiritual leader will choose the hidden pathway of sacrificial service and the approval of His Lord rather than the flamboyant assignment and the adulation of the unspiritual crowd.

In the early days of his ministry, one might have concluded that the greatness of John the Baptist lay in his fierce denunciation of the evils of his day, in the burning eloquence and blistering words that pierced and exposed the hearts of his contemporaries. But the secret that made him the greatest of those born of women is to be found in his unconscious but infinitely revealing affirmation: "He must increase, but I must decrease" (John 3:30). In that one sentence his spiritual stature is revealed.

The humility of the leader, as his spirituality, should be an ever-growing quality. It is instructive to notice Paul's advance in the grace of humility with the passing of the years. Early in his ministry, as he reviewed his past, and now abhorred, record, he acknowledged: "I am the least of the apostles, who am not fit to be called an apostle" (1 Cor. 15:9). Sometime later he volunteered: "[I am] the very least

of all saints" (Eph. 3:8). When his life was drawing
to a close and he was preparing to meet his Lord, he
mourned: "I am foremost of all [sinners]" (1 Tim.
1:15).

In his *Serious Call,* William Law exhorts:

> Let every day be a day of humility; conde-
> scend to all the weaknesses and infirmities of
> your fellow-creatures, cover their frailties, love
> their excellencies, encourage their virtues, re-
> lieve their wants, rejoice in their prosperities,
> compassionate their distress, receive their friend-
> ship, overlook their unkindness, forgive their
> malice, be a servant of servants, and condescend
> to do the lowliest offices of the lowest of man-
> kind.

On one occasion Samuel Brengle was introduced as
"the great Dr. Brengle." In his diary he wrote:

> If I appear great in their eyes, the Lord is
> most graciously helping me to see how abso-
> lutely nothing I am without Him, and helping me
> to keep little in my own eyes. He does use me.
> But I am so concerned that *He* uses me and that
> it is not of me the work is done. The axe can-
> not boast of the trees it has cut down. It could
> do nothing but for the woodsman. He made it,
> he sharpened it, and he used it. The moment he
> throws it aside, it becomes only old iron. O that
> I may never lose sight of this.[16]

The spiritual leader of today is in all probability
one who yesterday expressed his humility by working

gladly and faithfully in the second place. Out of his wisdom, Robert Morrison of China wrote: "The great fault, I think, in our missions is that no one likes to be second. Perhaps the advantages predominate, but I have not been able to see them."

INTEGRITY AND SINCERITY

Paul laid his heart bare in a way few of us are prepared to do—his failures as well as his successes. Even before his conversion he was sincere and a man of integrity who served God with a pure conscience (2 Tim. 1:3). Later he wrote to the Corinthians, "We are not like many, peddling the word of God, but as from sincerity . . . we speak in Christ in the sight of God" (2 Cor. 2:17). He did not shrink even from divine scrutiny (1 Cor. 4:4).

In the Old Testament, sincerity and integrity were enjoined on Israel (Deut. 18:13). Sincerity is transparency of character, an unconscious quality that is self-revealing.

In the early days of his ministry, Billy Graham was invited to an interview with Sir Winston Churchill. When he went to his appointment, to his dismay he found himself in the presence of the British cabinet. As he left the room after the interview, Churchill turned to his colleagues and said, "There goes a sincere man."

In reply to a question, a prominent businessman said, "If I had to name the one most important quality of a top manager, I would say, *personal integ-*

rity"—sincere in promise, faithful in discharge of duty, upright in finances, loyal in service, honest in speech.

NOTES

1. James Burns, *Revivals, Their Laws and Leaders* (London: Hodder & Stoughton, 1909), p. 182.
2. Phyllis Thompson, *Climbing on Track* (London: China Inland Mission, 1954), p. 116.
3. N. G. Dunning, *Samuel Chadwick* (London: Hodder & Stoughton, 1934), p. 15.
4. J. R. Andrews, *George Whitefield* (London: Morgan & Scott, 1915), pp. 410-11.
5. *World Vision,* January, 1966, p. 5.
6. Powhattan James, *George W. Truett* (Nashville: Broadman, 1953), p. 266.
7. Lettie B. Cowman, *Charles E. Cowman* (Los Angeles: Oriental Missionary Society, 1928), p. 259.
8. W. H. T. Gairdner, *Douglas M. Thornton* (London: Hodder & Stoughton, n.d.), p. 80.
9. Ibid., p. 43.
10. Marcus Loane, *Archbishop Mowll* (London: Hodder & Stoughton, 1960), p. 202.
11. Dunning, p. 20.
12. Theodore Roosevelt, in B. Matthews, *John R. Mott* (London: S. C. M. Press, 1934), p. 355.
13. Phyllis, Thompson, *D. E. Hoste* (London: China Inland Mission, n.d.), p. 155.
14. Burns, pp. 181-82.
15. Ibid., pp. 167-68.
16. C. W. Hall, *Samuel Logan Brengle* (New York: Salvation Army, 1933), p. 275.

9

QUALITIES ESSENTIAL TO LEADERSHIP—2

Deacons likewise must be men of dignity, not double-tongued, or addicted to much wine or fond of sordid gain, but holding to the mystery of the faith with a clear conscience. And let these also first be tested; then let them serve as deacons if they are beyond reproach.

1 TIMOTHY 3:8-10

HUMOR

Because man is in the image of God, his sense of humor is a gift of God and finds its counterpart in the divine nature. But it is a gift that is to be controlled as well as cultivated. Clean, wholesome humor will relax tension and relieve a difficult situation more than anything else. It can be of untold value in a leader, both for what it does for him and for the use it can be in his work. Humor can defuse a tense situation and restore a sense of the normal.

Samuel Johnson advised that a man should spend

part of his time with the laughters. Archbishop Whately, the great apologist, wrote: "We ought not only to cultivate the cornfield of the mind but the pleasure grounds also." Agnes Strickland claimed that "next to virtue, the fun in this world is what we can least spare."[1] A retired missionary was greatly dreading going to live in a home for retired missionaries. But in writing some months later, he said he had never been in a place where there was so much holy fun.

Charles H. Spurgeon was once chided for introducing humor into his preaching. With a twinkle in his eye he replied: "If only you knew how much I hold back, you would commend me." In justification of humorous touches in his pulpit, he wrote: "There are things in these sermons that may produce smiles, but what of them? The preacher is not quite sure about a smile being a sin, and at any rate he thinks it less a crime to cause a momentary laughter than a half-hour of profound slumber."

Helmut Thielecke wrote:

> Should we not see that lines of laughter about the eyes are just as much marks of faith as are the lines of care and seriousness? Is it only earnestness that is baptized? Is laughter pagan? We have already allowed too much that is good to be lost to the church and cast many pearls before swine. A church is in a bad way when it banishes laughter from the sanctuary and leaves it to the cabaret, the nightclub and the toastmasters.[2]

Humor is a great asset in missionary life. It is invaluable as a lubricant. Indeed it is a most serious deficiency if a missionary lacks a sense of humor. A Swede was urged by friends to give up the idea of returning to India as a missionary because it was so hot there. "Man," he was urged, "it is one hundred twenty degrees in the shade!"

"Vell," said the Swede in noble contempt, "ve don't always have to stay in the shade, do ve?"

A. E. Norrish, a missionary to India, testifies:

> "I have never met leadership without a sense of humor; this ability to stand outside oneself and one's circumstances, to see things in perspective and laugh. It is a great safety valve! You will never lead others far without the joy of the Lord and its concomitant, a sense of humor."[3]

Douglas Thornton was often more amusing than he tried to be. He had a delightful way of mixing up two kindred proverbs or idioms. Once he told his companions that he always had two strings up his sleeve. They then asked him if he also had another card to his bow. Such things enliven heavy committee meetings and create wholesome laughter.[4]

In half a century of experience as a minister, F. J. Hallett claimed he had found that in the actual work of a parish, the most successful man is he who possesses a keen sense of humor in combination with God's grace. Humor lends pungency, originality, and eloquence to sermons.

Of one great preacher it was said that he used
humor as a condiment and a stimulant. At times
paroxysms of laughter would rock his audiences, but
he never permitted sacred things to be involved. He
would quickly swing to the sublime, and his humor
did not degenerate into frivolity.

A good test of the appropriateness of our humor
is whether we control it or it controls us. Of Kenneth
Strachan, general director of the Latin America Mission, it was said: "He had a keen sense of humor,
but he had a sense of the fitness of things. He knew
the place for a joke and his humor was controlled."[5]

ANGER

Anger sounds like rather a strange qualification for
leadership. In another context it could be quoted as
a disqualifying factor. But was this quality not present
in the life of the supreme Leader? Jesus looked "on
them with anger" (Mark 3:5). Righteous wrath is
no less noble than love, since both coexist in God.
Each necessitates the other. It was Jesus' love for the
man with the withered hand that aroused His anger
against those who would deny him healing. It was
His love for His Father, and zeal for His glory, that
kindled His anger against the mercenary traders who
had turned His house of prayer for all nations into a
cave of robbers (Matt. 21:13, John 2:15-17).

Great leaders who have turned the tide in days of
national and spiritual declension have been men who
could get angry at the injustices and abuses that dis-
honor God and enslave men. It was righteous anger

against the heartless slave traders that caused Wilberforce to move heaven and earth for the emancipation of slaves.

F. W. Robertson was similarly stirred by righteous anger on one occasion. Describing his reaction he said: "My blood was at the moment running fire, and I remembered that once in my life I had felt a terrible might; I knew and rejoiced to know that I was inflicting the sentence of a coward's and a liar's hell."[6] Martin Luther claimed that he "never did anything well until his wrath was excited, and then he could do anything well."

But such anger is open to abuse, and few can entertain it without allowing it to degenerate into sin. Paul argues the possibility of righteous anger in his exhortation "Be angry and sin not." Holy anger is free from selfishness. Anger that centers upon self is always sinful. To be sinless it must be zeal for the rights of truth and purity, with the glory of God as its objective.

> Thou to wax fierce
> In the cause of the Lord!
> Anger and zeal
> And the joy of the brave,
> Who bade *thee* to feel,
> Sin's slave?
>
> AUTHOR UNKNOWN

Bishop Butler analyzed the conditions under which righteous wrath degenerates into sinful anger:

• When, from partiality to ourselves, we imagine an injury done to us when there is none

• When that partiality represents that injury to us greater than it really is

• When we feel resentment on account of pain or inconvenience without injury

• When indignation rises too high

• When pain or harm is inflicted to gratify that resentment, though naturally raised

When we are angry with sin in our own lives, we will be most likely to experience righteous anger at the sin in others.[7]

PATIENCE

A liberal endowment of patience is essential to sound leadership. Chrysostom called patience the Queen of Virtues. The popular use of the word is too passive to adequately convey its full significance in the original. William Barclay has this to say of its meaning as used in 2 Peter 1:6:

> The word never means the spirit which sits with folded hands and simply bears things. It is victorious endurance, masculine constancy under trial. It is Christian steadfastness, the brave and courageous acceptance of everything life can do to us, and the transmuting of even the worst into another step on the upward way. It is the courageous and triumphant ability to bear things, which enables a man to pass breaking point and not to break, and always to greet the unseen with a cheer."[8]

Patience does not mean passive acquiescence or submission to defeat. But it does mean forbearing with the slow learner.

It is in personal relationships that patience meets its most stringent test. Paul broke down in patience in his dealing with John Mark. Hudson Taylor once made this confession: "My greatest temptation is to lose my temper over the slackness and inefficiency so disappointing in those on whom I depended. It is no use to lose my temper—only kindness. But oh, it is such a trial."[9] Many other leaders experience the force of that temptation, but how clearly does it bring into relief the marvelous patience of our Lord with doubting Thomas, and unstable Peter, and traitorous Judas!

One manifestation of patience in a leader consists in his not running too far ahead of his followers and thus discouraging them. While keeping ahead, he stays near enough for them to keep him in sight and hear his call forward. He is not so strong that he cannot show a strengthening sympathy for the weakness of his fellows. "We who are strong *ought* to bear the weaknesses of those without strength" (Rom. 15:1, italics added). The man who is impatient with weakness will be defective in his leadership. The evidence of our strength lies not in racing ahead, but in a willingness to adapt our stride to the slower pace of our weaker brethren while not forfeiting our lead. If we run too far ahead, we lose our power to influence.

Of his father, Dr. A. J. Gordon, Ernest Gordon wrote:

Criticism and opposition he endured without recrimination. "A Christian should be a patient, undaunted, undiscouraged torchbearer for Christ. If a storm of abuse should chance to break on him, he is to stand in statue-like indifference to it all, holding forth the word of life. If blasts of ridicule dash him in the face, he is to take it silently and imperturbably as the bronze figure takes the tempest. It is the man who stands who moves the world."[10]

Patience is required when we seek to lead by persuasion rather than by command. Persuasion is the ability to get others to see one's viewpoint and act accordingly. We should cultivate the art of persuasion that lets the individual make his own decision.

Great patience may have to be exercised by a leader in the implementation of cherished plans that he believes to be in the best interests of the work for which he is responsible. D. E. Hoste said:

I shall never forget the impression made upon me by Hudson Taylor in connection with these affairs. Again and again he was obliged either to greatly modify or lay aside projects which were sound and helpful but met with determined opposition, and so tended to create greater evils than those which might have been removed or mitigated by the changes in question. Later on, in answer to patient continuance in prayer, many of such projects were given effect to."[11]

FRIENDSHIP

You can tell the stature of a leader by the number and the quality of his friends. Judged by that measuring rod, Paul had a genius for friendship. He was essentially a gregarious man. His relationship to Timothy is an example of an ideal friendship of an older for a young man, as is that with Luke of a friendship between contemporaries.

"The crowning glory of his leadership was that he was a friend of man. He loved the man next to him and he loved mankind."[12] That tribute to Dr. A. B. Simpson illustrates the fact that the spiritual leader will be a lover of men and will have a large capacity for friendship. David's peerless command of men sprang from his genius in gathering around him men of renown who were ready to die for him. So fully did he capture their affection and allegiance that a whispered wish was to them as a command (2 Sam. 23:15-16). They would die for him because they knew he would die for them.

"No man in the New Testament made fiercer enemies than Paul, but few men in the world have had better friends. They clustered around him so thickly that we are apt to lose their personality in their devotion."[13]

There are men like General Charles de Gaulle whose greatness is the greatness of isolation. On the contrary, Paul's greatness and successful leadership lay in no small measure in his ability to capture and to hold the intense love and loyalty of the friends with whom he freely mixed. True, he involved his friends in all sorts of risks for Christ's sake and the gospel's, but they followed him cheerfully because they were assured of his love for them. His letters glow with a

warmth of appreciation and personal affection for his
fellow workers.

Another important ingredient in leadership is the
faculty of being able to draw the best out of other
people. In achieving that, personal friendliness will
accomplish much more than prolonged and even successful argument. It was John R. Mott's counsel to
"rule by the heart. When logic and argument and
other forms of persuasion fail, fall back on the heart-
genuine friendship."

In his biography of Robert A. Jaffray, who played
a major part in opening Vietnam to the gospel, A. W.
Tozer pointed out that in one respect all spiritual
leaders have been alike. They have all had large
hearts. "Nothing can take the place of affection.
Those who have it in generous measure have a magic
power over men. Intellect will not do. Bible knowledge is not enough. Robert Jaffray loved people for
their own sakes. He was happy in the presence of
human beings, whatever their race and colour."[14]

Few have exercised in their own generation the
leadership in spiritual things wielded by Charles Had-
don Spurgeon. It was his biographer's conviction that
"he exercised an absolute authority, not because of
sheer wilfulness, though he was a wilful man, but because of his acknowledged worth. Men bowed to his
authority because it was authority backed by united
wisdom and affection."

One greater than David or Paul also ruled His followers by friendship and affection. Of Him it was
written, "Having loved his own who were in the world,

he loved them to the end" (John 13:1). It was the knowledge of that personal affection for him that at last broke Peter's heart and forced from him the confession: "You know all things; you know that I love you" (John 21:17).

TACT AND DIPLOMACY

The original meaning of *tact* was the sense of touch, and it came to mean skill in dealing with persons or sensitive situations. It is defined as "intuitive perception, especially a quick and fine perception of what is fit and proper and right; a ready appreciation of the proper thing to do or say, especially a fine sense of how to avoid giving offense."

Tact and diplomacy are closely related. *Diplomacy* is dexterity and skill in managing affairs of any kind, but as a result of abuses practiced by some who engage in the art, the word has become somewhat debased. Combining those two words, there emerges the idea of skill in reconciling opposing viewpoints without giving offense or compromising principle. They are invaluable qualities in the spiritual leader. He needs the imaginative projection of his own consciousness into the experience of the other person if he is to be able to help him. It is a quality that can be acquired and developed.

The ability to conduct delicate negotiations and matters concerning personnel in a way that recognizes mutual rights and yet leads to a harmonious solution is an asset greatly to be coveted. It involves the ability to place oneself in the position of the persons involved and to accurately assess how they would feel and react.

The same thing can be said in a tactful and in an untactful manner. One shoe salesman said to his client, "I'm sorry, madam, but your foot is too large for this shoe." The other salesman said to his client who was in a similar situation, "I'm sorry, madam, but this shoe is too small for your foot." Each used almost exactly the same words, but tact and diplomacy caused one to make a slightly different emphasis by a slight difference of phrasing, and secured a loyal and satisfied customer.

Joshua's division of the promised land among the Israelites affords an outstanding biblical example of the employment of tact and diplomacy. With a nation descended from scheming Jacob, such a delicate task in which human cupidity and greed were inevitably involved, held all the seeds of serious dissension and strife that could have rent the nation. The tactful manner in which Joshua was able to handle the transaction was evidence not only of human sagacity but of his close walk with God. The diplomacy he displayed in resolving the potentially bitter and explosive misunderstanding created by the tribes of Reuben and Gad's erecting another altar was further tribute not only to his native gift but to the wisdom he had learned in the school of God.

William Carey was unconsciously a diplomat. One of his fellow workers testified of him: "He has attained the happy art of ruling and overruling others without asserting his authority, or others feeling their subjection—and all is done without the least appearance of design on his part."[15] Tact and diplomacy are never more effective than when they are unconscious and unstudied.

INSPIRATIONAL POWER

The power of inspiring others to service and sacrifice will mark God's leader. His incandescence sets those around him alight. Charles Cowman not only achieved a prodigious amount of work himself but possessed the ability to inject the spirit of work into those with whom he was associated. His zeal and drive were infectious.[16]

Pastor Hsi was one of the truly great Christian leaders of his day in China. He, too, possessed that capacity to an extraordinary degree. One who was closely linked with him in the service of the Lord was asked, "Did you notice about him any special aptitude for leading and influencing others?" He replied, "His power in that direction was remarkable; without any effort, apparently, he seemed to sway everybody. Instinctively people followed and trusted him. Then, too, he possessed great power of initiative and an energy and enterprise that were extraordinary. One could not be with him without gaining a wholly new ideal of Christian life and service."[17]

Nehemiah also displayed that power in abundant measure. When he arrived in Jerusalem the people were utterly disheartened and dispirited. In no time he succeeded in welding them into an aggressive and effective working force. Such was his power to in-

spire that before long we read, "The people had a
mind to work." It would be true to say that work on
the walls would not have been commenced, much less
completed, apart from the inspiration imparted by
Nehemiah.

General Mark Clark, in addressing a class of train-
ees, once said of Sir Winston Churchill: "I doubt if
any man in history has ever made such grim utter-
ances, yet given his people such a sense of strength,
exuberance, even of cheerfulness."

When France fell to the German armies and Britain
was left alone in the fight, the British cabinet met in
a sense of deep gloom—for which there was abundant
reason. When Winston Churchill entered, he looked
around at his disconsolate colleagues and said, "Gentlemen, I find this rather inspiring." Small wonder
that he was able to galvanize the nation into effective counterattack.

EXECUTIVE ABILITY

One who lacks executive ability to any considerable
degree, however clearly he may see things spiritual,
will be unable to translate his vision into action. It
is true that subtle dangers lie in overmuch organization, for it can be a very unsatisfactory substitute for
the presence and working of the Holy Spirit. But that
is not necessarily so. Lack of method and organization has its dangers too and has spelled failure for
many a promising venture for God.

In his *Book of Isaiah,* Sir George Adam Smith calls

attention to the word ambiguously translated "judgment" in the King James Version and reminds us that it means "method, order, system, law." So when Isaiah says, "The LORD is a God of judgment" (30: 18), he means, among other things, that God is a God of method. His creation is superbly ordered. Because He is a God of order, He requires of those whom He entrusts with leadership "that all things be done decently and in order." "It is a great truth," Smith writes, "that the Almighty and All-merciful is the All-methodical too. No religion is complete in its creed, or healthy in its influence, which does not insist equally on all these."[18]

It is for us to emulate the orderliness and method of God in our own work for Him. Although it is true that men cannot be organized into the kingdom, that does not justify the absence of careful planning, in dependence on the Spirit's leading, and skillful execution of what has been planned for their salvation.

Lord Macaulay said that Wesley had a genius for government not inferior to that of Richelieu. The genius of his organization is still seen in the church that he founded. It is owing to his superb executive ability and powers of organization that the movement remained unshaken even when deprived of his presence and guidance.

His judgment of men, his skill in using them, his power to employ them to the best advantage and to attach them to himself in loyal submission amounted to genius and saved the movement from the most serious dangers.[19]

THE THERAPY OF LISTENING

A sympathetic ear is a valuable asset. The art of listening is one that must be mastered if the leader is to get at the root of the problem to be solved. Too many are compulsive talkers. "He won't listen to me," complained one missionary. "He is giving the answer before I have had a chance to really state the problem."

To many, listening is often the impatient waiting until one can get his views across. But listening is a genuine effort to understand what the other person has to say and to do it without prejudging the issue. A problem is often half solved when it is stated. One missionary who became a casualty moaned, "If only he had listened to me. I needed someone with whom I could share my problem."

Sensitivity to another's needs is expressed more by listening than by talking. Leaders frequently give the impression, often unconsciously, that they are too busy to listen. Happy the man who gives the impression that there is ample time to hear the problem. Time spent listening is well invested.

When a prospective politician approached Justice Oliver Wendell Holmes, asking how to get elected to office, he replied: "To be able to listen to others in a sympathetic and understanding manner, is perhaps the most effective mechanism in the world for getting along with people, and tying up their friendship for good. Too few people practise the 'white magic' of being good listeners."[20]

THE ART OF LETTER WRITING

Any position of leadership involves a considerable amount of correspondence, and letters are self-revealing. We know more of the real Paul from his letters than from any historical material. His letters are models for the spiritual leader. They combine felicity of expression, freshness of thought, moral integrity, and intellectual honesty. When a difficult letter had to be written, he dipped his pen in tears, not in acid. "For out of much affliction and anguish of heart I wrote to you with many tears" (2 Cor. 2:4).

After he had written a strong letter to the erring Corinthians, his tender heart caused him to wonder if he had been too severe. "For though I caused you sorrow by my letter, I do not regret it; though I did regret it—for I see that that letter caused you to sorrow . . . I now rejoice . . . that you were made sorrowful to the point of repentance" (2 Cor. 7:8-9). In writing such a letter, his objective was not to win an argument but to resolve a spiritual problem and produce a growing maturity.

Paul's letters abounded in encouragement, were gracious in compliment and rich in sympathy. The recipients were always enriched (e.g., Phil. 1:27-30). But that did not restrain him from being faithful in correcting faults. "Have I therefore become your enemy by telling you the truth? . . . But I could wish to be present with you now and to change my tone, for I am perplexed about you" (Gal. 4:16, 20).

It is important to couch our letters in clear speech

so that the meaning is clear, but it is more important to have them breathing the right spirit. Letters are an unsatisfactory medium of communication. They cannot smile when they are saying something difficult, and therefore additional care should be taken to see that they are warm in tone.

Letters formed an important part in Paul's program of follow-up. It was said of George Whitefield that after preaching to large crowds, he would sometimes stay up until 3:00 A.M. writing letters of encouragement to new converts.

NOTES

1. C. W. Hall, *Samuel Logan Brengle* (New York: Salvation Army, 1933), p. 278.
2. Helmut Thielecke, *Encounter with Spurgeon* (Philadelphia: Fortress, 1963), p. 26.
3. A. E. Norrish, *Christian Leadership* (New Delhi: Masihi Sabiyata Sanstha, 1963), p. 28.
4. W. H. T. Gairdner, *Douglas M. Thornton* (London: Hodder & Stoughton, n.d.), p. 84.
5. *Latin America Evangelist,* May-June, 1965.
6. Robert E. Speer, *Christ and Life* (New York: Revell, 1901), p. 103.
7. Ibid., p. 104.
8. William Barclay, *Letters of Peter and Jude* (Edinburgh: St. Andrews, 1960), p. 258.
9. J. C. Pollock, *Hudson Taylor and Maria* (London: Hodder & Stoughton, 1962), p. 35.
10. Ernest Gordon, *A. J. Gordon* (London: Hodder & Stoughton, 1897), p. 191.
11. Phyllis Thompson, *D. E. Hoste* (London: China Inland Mission, n.d.), p. 158.
12. A. E. Thompson, *The Life of A. B. Simpson* (Harrisburg: Christian Publications, 1920), p. 204.
13. H. C. Lees, *St. Paul's Friends* (London: Religious Tract Society, 1917), p. 11.
14. A. W. Tozer, *Let My People Go* (Harrisburg: Christian Publications, 1957), p. 36.

15. S. P. Carey, *William Carey* (London: Hodder & Stoughton, 1923), p. 256.
16. Lettie B. Cowman, *Charles E. Cowman* (Los Angeles: Oriental Missionary Society, 1928), p. 269.
17. Mrs. Hudson Taylor, *Pastor Hsi* (London: China Inland Mission, 1949), pp. 164, 167.
18. George Adam Smith, *The Book of Isaiah* (London: Hodder & Stoughton, n.d.), p. 229.
19. James Burns, *Revival, Their Laws and Leaders* (London: Hodder & Stoughton, 1909), p. 311.
20. *World Vision,* February 1966, p. 5.

10

THE INDISPENSABLE REQUIREMENT

*Select . . . seven men . . . full of the Spirit. . . .
And they chose Stephen, a man full of . . . the
Holy Spirit.*

ACTS 6:3, 5

Spiritual leadership can be exercised only by Spirit-filled men. Other qualifications for spiritual leadership are desirable. To be Spirit-filled is indispensable.

The book of Acts, an inspired source book for principles of leadership, is the story of the men who established the Christian church and led the missionary enterprise. It is of more than passing significance that the central qualification of those who were to occupy even subordinate positions of responsibility in the early church was that they be men "full of the Holy Spirit." They must be known by their integrity and sagacity, but preeminently for their spirituality. However brilliant a man may be intellectually, however capable an administrator, without that essential equipment he is incapable of giving truly spiritual leadership.

Behind the actions of the apostles, the executive activity of the Spirit is seen everywhere. As supreme Administrator of the church and chief Strategist of the missionary enterprise, He is everywhere prominent. It is abundantly evident in the record that the Holy Spirit is jealous of His prerogatives and will not delegate His power or authority to secular or carnal hands. Even men whose duties would be largely in the temporal affairs of the church must be men mastered and controlled by Him. Their selection must not be influenced by considerations of worldly wisdom, financial acumen, or social acceptability; they should be chosen primarily because of their genuine spirituality. When a church or other Christian organization departs from that pattern, it amounts to a virtual ousting of the Spirit from His place of leadership. As a consequence He is grieved and quenched, with resulting spiritual dearth and death.

Choosing men for office in the church or any of its auxiliaries without reference to spiritual qualifications must of necessity result in an unspiritual administration. In illustrating such a situation, Dr. A. T. Pierson likened that to the course sometimes pursued in a large company when it desires to rid itself of its controlling head. Gradually, in the subordinate offices and in the board of trustees, or directors, men are introduced who are opposed to the presiding officer in method and spirit. They quietly antagonize his measures, obstruct his plans, thwart his policy. Instead of cooperation and support, he meets inertia and indifference, if not violent opposition, until at last, unable to conduct affairs, he resigns from sheer inability to carry out his policy of administration.[1] Appointment of men with a secular or materialistic outlook prevents the Holy Spirit from carrying out His program for the church in the world.

The Holy Spirit does not take control of any man or body of men against their will. When He sees elected to positions of leadership men who lack spiritual fitness to cooperate with Him, He quietly withdraws and leaves them to implement their own policy according to their own standards, but without His aid. The inevitable issue is an unspiritual administration.

The church at Jerusalem was sensitive to the exhortation of the apostles and selected seven men possessing the requisite qualities. As a result of their Spirit-filled activity, the disaffection was quickly healed, the church was blessed, and the men selected to dispense earthly benefits were soon seen as the Spirit's agents in dispensing heavenly blessings. Stephen became the first martyr for Christ, and his death played no small part in the conversion of Saul. Philip became the first lay evangelist and was used by the Spirit to lead the great revival in Samaria. Faithfulness in the exercise of gifts of nature and grace prepares the way for elevation to greater planes of usefulness and, perhaps, the multiplication of those gifts.

It stands clear in the book of Acts that the leaders

who significantly influenced the Christian movement were men who were filled with the Holy Spirit. It is recorded of Him who commanded His disciples to tarry in Jerusalem until they were endued with power from on high that He was Himself "anointed . . . with the Holy Spirit and with power" (10:38). The privileged one hundred twenty in the upper room were all filled with the Spirit (2:4). Peter was filled with the Spirit when he addressed the Sanhedrin (4:8). Stephen, filled with the Spirit, was enabled to bear irresistible witness to Christ and to die as a radiant martyr (6:3, 5; 7:55). It was in the Spirit's fullness that Paul commenced and exercised his unique ministry (9:17; 13:9). His missionary companion Barnabas was filled with the Spirit (11:24). He would be strangely blind who did not discern in that fact the fundamental criterion and equipment for spiritual leadership.

Those men were very sensitive to the overriding leading of the Holy Spirit. Because they had willingly submitted to His control, they were delighted to obey His promptings and leadings. Philip left the flourishing revival in Samaria without demur, at the Spirit's prompting, accepting instead designation to a desert. But what a fish he was to catch in the desert (8:29)! It was the Spirit who overcame Peter's reluctance and led him to Cornelius, with incalculable blessings resulting for the Gentile world (10:19; 11:12). The Spirit called and sent out Saul and Barnabas as the first missionaries (13:1-4). In his missionary travels, Paul was obedient to the restraints as well as the con-

straints of the Spirit (16:6-7; 19:21; 20:22). The
recognized leaders of the church, meeting in council
at Jerusalem, deferred to the leading of the Spirit.
"It seemed good to the Holy Spirit and to us" was the
way in which the findings of the council were promul-
gated (15:28).

It should be noted that each of the interventions
of the Holy Spirit had as its objective the bringing of
the gospel to the Gentiles. His great preoccupation,
then as now, was to make the church a missionary
church. Should His preoccupation not be ours too?

One of the most encouraging features of missionary
work in East Asia at the time of writing is the moving
of the Spirit in some of the Asian churches, imparting
to them a new missionary vision and passion. For
instance, the Japanese churches have sent out hundreds of their own number as foreign missionaries to
countries as widely separated as Taiwan and Brazil.
At a time when the missionary force from Western
lands has become numerically static, the heavenly
Strategist is awaking the Asian church to her missionary obligations. There are at this time more than
three thousand Third World Christians who, at the
call of God, have become bona fide cross-cultural missionaries.

Paul's counsel to the church leaders at Ephesus
throws an illuminating sidelight on the way in which
their office should be viewed. "Be on guard for yourselves, and for all the flock, among which the Holy
Spirit has made you overseers" (20:28). They did
not hold their office by apostolic selection or popular

election, but by divine appointment. They are answerable not to the church alone, but also to the Holy Spirit. What a sense of assurance and responsibility, what a spiritual authority that consciousness would impart to them!

The purposes of the Spirit's filling at Pentecost were eminently practical. The apostles were faced with a superhuman task for which nothing less than supernatural power would avail. The fullness of the Spirit imparted the power they needed for the truceless warfare to which they were committed (Luke 24: 29; Eph. 6:10-18).

Reduced to its simplest terms, to be filled with the Spirit means that, through voluntary surrender and in response to appropriating faith, the human personality is filled, mastered, controlled by the Holy Spirit. The very word *filled* supports that meaning. The idea is not that of something being poured into a passive empty receptacle. "That which takes possession of the mind is said to fill it," says Thayer, the great lexicographer. That usage of the word is found in Luke 5:26 (KJV): "They were filled with fear," and in John 16:6: "Because I have said these things to you, sorrow has filled your heart." Their fear and sorrow possessed them to the exclusion of other emotions; they mastered and controlled them. That is what the Holy Spirit does when we invite Him to fill us.

To be filled with the Spirit, then, is to be controlled by the Spirit. Intellect and emotions and volition as well as physical powers all become available to Him for achieving the purposes of God. Under His control, natural gifts of leadership are sanctified and lifted to their highest power. The now ungrieved and unhindered Spirit is able to produce the fruit of the Spirit in the life of the leader, with added winsomeness and attractiveness in his service and with power in his witness to Christ. All real service is but the effluence of the Holy Spirit through yielded and filled lives (John 7:37-39).

A. W. Tozer had clear insight into the possibility of superficiality in seeking after that experience when he said:

> No one whose senses have been exercised to know good and evil can but grieve over the sight of zealous souls seeking to be filled with the Holy Spirit while they are living in a state of moral carelessness and borderline sin. Whoever would be indwelt by the Spirit must judge his life for any hidden iniquities. He must expel from his heart everything that is out of accord with the character of God as revealed by the Holy Scriptures. . . . There can be no tolerance of evil, no laughing off the things that God hates.[2]

The fullness of the Spirit is an essential and indispensable experience for spiritual leadership. And each of us is as full of the Spirit as we really want to be.

SPIRITUAL GIFTS

We are surrounded by Christians who have undiscovered or underutilized spiritual gifts. It is the responsibility of the leader to discover those and to aid in their development. Spirituality alone does not make a leader, there must be the appropriate gifts of nature and of grace.

In our warfare against a supernatural spiritual foe, we need supernatural equipment, and God has provided that in the spiritual gifts He has given to His church. It should be said that the effective exercise of any spiritual gift must be preceded by the enrichment of spiritual grace.

Generally, though not always, the Holy Spirit imparts gifts that the recipient is naturally fitted to exercise, but He raises them to a new effectiveness. Samuel Chadwick, the noted Methodist preacher, once said that when he was filled with the Spirit, he did not receive a new set of brains, but a new mentality; not a new faculty of speech, but a new effectiveness; not a new dictionary, but a new Bible. The same basis of natural qualities were vitalized and energized to a degree never before experienced.

Spiritual gifts do not supersede natural gifts, but they do enhance and stimulate them. The new birth does not change natural qualities, but when those are placed under the control of the Holy Spirit, they are raised to a new effectiveness. Hidden abilities are often released.

The one who is called of God to leadership can confidently expect that the Holy Spirit has endowed him with the requisite spiritual gifts, for their purpose is to qualify the possessor for that ministry to the Body of Christ that has been assigned to him. It is worthy of note that not one of the spiritual gifts refers di-

rectly to character. They are in the main gifts for
service.

NOTES

1. A. T. Pierson, *The Acts of the Holy Spirit* (London: Morgan
   & Scott, n.d.), p. 63.
2. D. J. Fant, *A. W. Tozer* (Harrisburg: Christian Publications,
   1964), pp. 73, 83.

11

THE LEADER AND HIS PRAYING

First of all, . . . entreaties and prayers, petitions and thanksgivings . . .

1 TIMOTHY 2:1

In nothing should the leader be ahead of his followers more than in the realm of prayer. And yet the most advanced Christian is conscious of the possibility of endless development in his prayer life. Nor does he ever feel that he has "already attained." Dean C. J. Vaughan once said: "If I wished to humble anyone, I should question him about his prayers. I know nothing to compare with this topic for its sorrowful self-confessions."

Prayer is the most ancient, most universal, most intense expression of the religious instinct. It touches infinite extremes, for it is at once the simplest form of speech that infant lips can try and the sublimest strains that reach the Majesty on high. It is indeed the Christian's vital breath and native air.

But, strange paradox, most of us are plagued with a subtle aversion to praying. We do not naturally delight in drawing near to God. We pay lip service to the delight and potency and value of prayer. We assert that it is an indispensable adjunct of mature spiritual life. We know that it is constantly enjoined and exemplified in the Scriptures. But in spite of all, too often we fail to pray.

Let us take encouragement from the lives of men of like passions with ourselves who have conquered their natural reluctance and become mighty men of prayer.

The biographer of Samuel Chadwick wrote:

> He was essentially a man of prayer. Every morning he would be astir shortly after six o'clock, and he kept a little room which was his private sanctum for his quiet hour before breakfast. He was mighty in public prayer because he was constant in private devotion. . . . When he prayed he expected God to do something. "I wish I had prayed more," he wrote toward the end of his life, "even if I had worked less; and from the bottom of my heart I wish I had prayed better."[1]

"When I go to prayer," confessed an eminent Christian, "I find my heart so loath to go to God, and when it is with Him, so loath to stay." It is just at that point that self-discipline must be exercised. "When thou feelest most indisposed to pray, yield not to it," he counseled, "but strive and endeavour to pray, even when thou thinkest thou canst not pray."

Mastering the art of prayer, like any other art, will take time, and the amount of time we allocate to it will be the true measure of our conception of its importance. We always contrive to find time for that which we deem most important. To most, crowding duties are a reason for curtailing time spent in prayer. To busy Martin Luther, extra work was a compelling argument for spending *more* time in prayer. Hear his answer to an inquiry about his plans for the next day's work: "Work, work from early till late. In fact I have so much to do that I shall spend the first three hours in prayer." If our view of the importance of prayer in any degree approximates that of Luther and Luther's Lord, we will somehow make more time for it.

It is of course true that prayer poses intellectual problems. But those who are skeptical of its validity and efficacy are usually those who do not seriously put it to the test, or who fail to comply with the revealed conditions. There is no way to learn to pray except by praying. No reasoned philosophy by itself ever taught a soul to pray. But to the man who fulfills the conditions, the problems are met in the indisputable fact of answered prayer and the joy of conscious fellowship with God.

For the supreme example of a life of prayer, the leader will naturally turn to the life of the Lord Himself, since belief in the rationality and necessity of prayer is based not merely on logic but preeminently on His example and precept. If prayer could have been dispensed with in any life, surely it would have been in that of the sinless Son of Man. If prayer was unnecessary or unreasonable, we would naturally expect it to be omitted from His life and teaching. On the contrary, it was the dominant feature of His life and a recurrent element in His teaching. An examination of its incidence reveals that prayer kept the vision of His moral duty sharp and clear. It was prayer that nerved Him to do and endure the perfect but costly will of His Father. Prayer paved the way for the transfiguration. To Him, prayer was not a reluctant addendum, but a joyous necessity.

D. M. McIntyre wrote:

> In Luke 5:16 we have a general statement which throws a vivid light on the daily practice of the Lord. "And He withdrew Himself in the deserts and prayed." It is not of one occasion but of many that the evangelist speaks in this place. It was our Lord's habit to seek retirement for prayer. When He withdrew Himself from men, He was accustomed to press far into the uninhabited country—He was *in the deserts*. The surprise of the onlookers lay in this, that one so mighty, so richly endowed with spiritual power, should find it necessary for Himself to repair to the source of strength, that there He might refresh His weary spirit. To us, the wonder is still greater, that He, the Prince of Life, the Eternal Word, the Only-begotten of the Father, should prostrate Himself in meekness before the throne of God, making entreaty for grace to help in time of need.[2]

Christ used to spend nights in prayer (Luke 6:12). He often rose a great while before day in order to have unbroken communion with His Father (Mark 1:35). The great crises of His life and ministry were preceded by special prayer (e.g., Luke 5:16), "He Himself would often slip away to the wilderness and pray," a statement that indicated a regular habit. Both by word and example He impressed upon His disciples the importance of solitude in prayer (Mark 6:46; Luke 9:28). To the man on whom devolves the responsibility for selecting personnel for specific spiritual responsibilities, the example of the Lord in His choice of His disciples is luminous.

Both our Lord and His bondslave Paul made clear that true prayer is not pleasant dreamy reverie. "All vital praying makes a drain on a man's vitality. True intercession is a sacrifice, a bleeding sacrifice," wrote J. H. Jowett. Jesus performed many mighty works without outward sign of strain, but of His praying it is recorded, "He offered up both prayers and supplications with strong crying and tears" (Heb. 5:7).

How pale a reflection of Paul's and Epaphras's strivings and wrestlings are our pallid and languid intercessions! "Epaphras . . . laboring earnestly for you in his prayers," wrote Paul to the believers at Colossae (4:12). And to the same group, " I would that ye knew how great conflict I have for you" (2:1, KJV). The word for "wrestling," "conflict," is that from which our "agonize" is derived. It is used of a man toiling at his work until utterly weary (Col. 1:

29), or competing in the arena for the coveted prize (1 Cor. 9:25). It describes the soldier battling for his life (1 Tim. 6:12), or a man struggling to deliver his friend from danger (John 18:36). From those and other considerations it is clear that true praying is a strenuous spiritual exercise that demands the utmost mental discipline and concentration.

It is encouraging to recall that Paul, probably the greatest human exponent and example of the exercise of prayer, confessed, "We do not know how to pray as we should." But he hastened to add, "The Spirit also helps our weakness . . . but the Spirit Himself intercedes for us with groanings too deep for words; and He who searches the hearts knows what the mind of the Spirit is, because He intercedes for the saints according to the will of God" (Rom. 8:26-28). The Spirit links Himself with us in our praying and pours His supplications into our own.

We may master the technique of prayer and understand its philosophy; we may have unlimited confidence in the veracity and validity of the promises concerning prayer; we may plead them earnestly. But if we ignore the part played by the Holy Spirit, we have failed to use the master key.

Progressive teaching in the art of praying is needed, and the Holy Spirit is the master Teacher. His assistance in prayer is more frequently mentioned in Scripture than any of His other offices. All true praying stems from His activity in the soul. Both Paul and Jude teach that effective prayer is "praying in the Spirit." The phrase has been interpreted as praying along the same lines, about the same things, in the same name, as the Holy Spirit. True prayer rises in the spirit of the Christian from the Spirit who indwells him.

"Praying in the Spirit" may have a dual significance. It may mean praying *in the realm of the Spirit,* for the Holy Spirit is the sphere and atmosphere of the Christian's life. But in fact, many of our prayers are *psychical* rather than spiritual. They move in the realm of the mind alone, the product of our own thinking and not of the Spirit's teaching. But it is something deeper. The type of praying envisaged in that phrase "utilizes the body, demands the cooperation of the mind, but moves in the supernatural realm of the Spirit." That kind of prayer transacts its business in the heavenly realm.

But the phrase "praying in the Spirit" may also mean praying *in the power and energy of the Spirit.* "Give yourselves wholly to prayer and entreaty; pray on every occasion in the power of the Spirit," is the *New English Bible* rendering of Ephesians 6:18. For its superhuman task, prayer demands more than mere human power, and that is supplied by the Holy Spirit. He is the Spirit of power as well as the Spirit of prayer. Human energy of heart and mind and will can achieve only human results, but praying in the Holy Spirit releases supernatural resources.

It is the Spirit's delight to aid the man entrusted with spiritual leadership in his moral and physical weakness in the matter of prayer, for the praying soul labors under three handicaps. But in each of them he may count upon the Spirit's assistance. Sometimes he is kept from prayer by the conscious *iniquity of his heart*. As he trusts Him, the Holy Spirit will lead and enable him to appropriate the cleansing of that mighty solvent, the blood of Christ. Then the spiritual leader is hampered by the *ignorance of his mind*. The Spirit, who knows the mind of God, will share that knowledge with him as he receptively waits on Him. He does that by imparting a clear conviction that a petition is or is not according to the will of God. Again, the spiritual leader will often be earthbound through the benumbing *infirmity of his body,* and especially so if he lives in the enervating climate of the tropics. The Spirit will quicken his mortal body in response to his faith and will enable him to rise above adverse physical and climatic conditions.

In addition to those personal handicaps, the praying man has to overcome the subtle opposition of Satan who will seek to oppress or depress, to create doubt or discouragement. In the Holy Spirit the praying man has been given a heavenly ally against a supernatural adversary.

The foregoing thoughts are doubtless not new ground to many who have read them, but is the mighty assistance, the power, of the Spirit in prayer a present and enjoyed experience? Have we slipped into an unintentional independence of the Spirit in prayer? Are we habitually "praying in the Spirit" and receiving the full answer to our prayers? It is very easy for our intellectual apprehension of spiritual truths to outrun our practical experience of their reality and power.

Prayer is frequently represented in Scripture under the figure of spiritual warfare. "Our struggle is . . . against the rulers, against powers, against the world forces of this darkness, against the spiritual forces of wickedness in the heavenly places" (Eph. 6:12). In that phase of the prayer life, three personalities are involved, not two. Between God on the one hand and the devil on the other, stands the praying man. Though weak in himself, he occupies a strategic role in the deathless struggle between the dragon and the Lamb. The power and authority he wields are not inherent, but are delegated to him by the victorious Christ to whom he is united by faith. His faith is the reticulating system through which the victory gained on Calvary over Satan and his hosts reaches the captives and delivers them.

Throughout the gospels, the thoughtful reader will discern that Jesus was concerned not so much with the wicked men and the evil conditions He confronted as with the forces of evil at the back of them. Behind well-meaning and ever-vocal Peter, behind the traitorous Judas, Jesus saw the black hand of Satan. "Get thee behind me, Satan," was the Lord's response to Peter's well-intentioned but presumptuous rebuke. We see men around us bound in sin and in captivity to the devil, but our concern in prayer should be not only *to pray for them* but *to pray against Satan* who holds them captive. He must be compelled to relax his grip on them, and that can be achieved only by Christ's victory on the cross. Jesus dealt with the cause rather than the effect, and the leader should adopt the same method in that aspect of his praying. And he must know how to lead those under him to victory in that spiritual warfare.

In a graphic illustration, Jesus likened Satan to a strong man, fully armed, who kept his palace and goods in peace. Before he could be dispossessed and his captives released, Jesus said he must first be bound, or rendered powerless. Only then could the rescue be effected (Matt. 12:28-29). What does it mean to "bind the strong man" if not to neutralize his power by drawing on the conquering power of Christ, who was manifested "to destroy [nullify, render inoperative] the works of the devil"? And how can that be done but by the prayer of faith, which lays hold on the victory of Calvary and believes for its repetition in the specific context of the prayer? We must not make the mistake of reversing our Lord's order and expect to effect the rescue without first disarming the adversary. The divinely delegated authority placed in our hands may be confidently exercised, for did not our Lord say to His weak disciples, "Behold, I have given you authority . . . over all the power of the enemy" (Luke 10:19)?

Because leadership is the ability to move and influence people, the spiritual leader will be alert to discover the most effective way of doing that. One of the most frequently quoted of Hudson Taylor's statements is his expression of conviction that "it is possible to move men, through God, *by prayer alone.*" In the course of his missionary career he demonstrated its truth a thousand times. However, it is one thing to give mental assent to his motto, but quite another thing consistently to put it into practice. Men are difficult objects to move, and it is much easier to pray for temporal needs than for situations that involve the intricacies and stubbornness of the human heart. But it is in just such situations that the leader must prove his power to move human hearts in the direction in which he believes the will of God lies. And God has placed in his hands the key to that complicated lock.

It is the supreme dignity and glory of man that he can say no as well as yes to the omnipotent God, for he has been endowed with the Godlike quality of free will. That fact poses a genuine problem to the student of the subject of prayer. If by our prayers we can affect the conduct of a fellowman, does that not trespass upon his free will? Will God violate one person's free will in order to answer another person's prayer? And yet, if our prayers cannot so influence Him, what is the point in praying?

In considering the problem, the first thing to remember is that *God is always consistent with Himself in His actions.* He does not contradict Himself. If He promises to answer the prayer of faith, He will do so, but not in a manner that would be contrary to His divine nature. He will fulfill all His obligations, but in a way consistent with His own attributes and undertakings, for "he cannot deny himself." No word or action will contradict any other word or action.

Then there is the indisputable fact that *intercessory prayer is a divine ordinance.* Since God has ordained it, we can be confident that as we fulfill the revealed conditions, the answer will most surely be granted, despite any seeming problems that might be involved. God obviously sees no insuperable problem or contradiction between human free will and His answering prayer. When He commands us to pray "for kings and those that are in authority," there is implicit in the command the assurance that our prayers can move them and significantly influence the course of events. Else, why pray? Whether or not we find a final mental answer to our prayer problems, we are still under obligation to pray.

Further, *we can know the will of God* concerning the subject of the prayer we offer, and that fact constitutes the basis for our being able to pray the prayer of faith. God can speak to us very convincingly through the channel of our own faculties. We have the Word of God, which presents the will of God on all matters of principle. We have the ministry of the Holy Spirit in our hearts, interceding for us according to the will of God (Rom. 8:26-27). As we patiently seek to discover God's will concerning our petition, the Spirit will impress us whether or not it is the will of God. It is that God-given conviction that enables us to proceed beyond the prayer of hope to the prayer of faith.

The very fact that God lays a burden of prayer on our hearts and keeps us praying is prima facie evidence that He purposes to grant the answer. When asked if he really believed that two men for whose salvation he had prayed for over fifty years would be converted, George Mueller of Bristol replied, "Do you think God would have kept me praying all these years if He did not intend to save them?" Both men were converted, one shortly before, the other after, Mueller's death.

In prayer, we deal directly with God and only in a secondary sense with men and women. The goal of prayer is the ear of God. Prayer influences men by influencing God to influence them. It is not the prayer that moves men, but the God to whom we pray.

> Prayer moves the arm
> That moves the world
> To bring deliverance down.
>
> AUTHOR UNKNOWN

To move men, the leader must be able to move God, for He has made it clear that He moves them through the prayers of the intercessor. If a scheming Jacob could be given "power with God and with men," then is it not possible for any leader who is willing to comply with the conditions to enjoy the same power (Gen. 32:28)?

Prevailing prayer of that kind is the outcome of a correct relationship with God. Reasons for unanswered prayer are stated with great clarity in Scripture, and they all center on the believer's relationship with God. He will not be party to petitions of mere self-interest, nor will He countenance impurity of motive. Sin clung to and cherished will effectively close His ear. Least of all will He tolerate unbelief, the mother of sins. "He who comes to God *must believe*" (Heb. 11:6, italics added). Everywhere in prayer there is the condition, either expressed or implied, that the paramount motive in praying is the glory of God.

The eminence of great leaders of the Bible is attributable to the fact that they were great in their praying. "They were not leaders because of brilliancy of thought, because they were exhaustless in resources, because of their magnificent culture or native endowment, but because, by the power of prayer, they could comand the power of God."[3]

NOTES

1. N. G. Dunning, *Samuel Chadwick* (London: Hodder & Stoughton, 1934), p. 19.
2. D. M. McIntyre, *The Prayer Life of Our Lord* (London: Morgan & Scott, n.d.), pp. 30-31.
3. E. M. Bounds, *Prayer and Praying Men* (London: Hodder & Stoughton, 1921).

12

THE LEADER AND HIS TIME

Make . . . the most of your time.

EPHESIANS 5:16

Time has been defined as a stretch of duration in which things happen. The quality of a man's leadership is revealed in what happens during that stretch of duration. The character and career of a young person are determined largely by how and with whom he spends his spare time. He cannot regulate school or office hours—those are determined for him—but he can say what he will do before and after. The manner in which he employs the surplus hours after provision has been made for work, meals, and sleep will make him either a mediocrity or a man to be reckoned with. Habits are formed in youth that make or mar a life. Leisure hours constitute a glorious opportunity or a subtle danger. Each moment of the day is a gift from God and should be husbanded with miserly care, for time is life measured out to us for work.

Minutes and hours can be transmuted into rich and abundant life. Michelangelo grasped that fact. On one occasion when he was executing a work that he had been pressured into doing, someone warned him, "It may cost your life." The great artist responded, "What else is life for?" Our hours and days will keep on being used up, but they can be used purposefully and productively. Philosopher William James affirmed that the great use of one's life is to spend it for something that will outlast it, for the value of life is computed not by its duration but by its donation. Not how long we live, but how fully and how well.

Yet in spite of its preciousness and vast potentialities, there is nothing that we squander so thoughtlessly as time. Moses considered it so invaluable a commodity that he prayed to be taught to measure it by days, not years (Psalm 90:12). If we are meticulously careful in the use of the days, the years will take care of themselves.

A sentence that will seldom be heard on the lips of a leader is "I don't have the time." Very seldom is it strictly true. It is usually the refuge of the small and inefficient person. We have each been entrusted with sufficient time to do the whole will of God and to fill out His perfect plan for our lives. "I think one of the cant phrases of our day is the familiar one by which we express our permanent want of time," said Dr. J. H. Jowett. "We repeat it so often that by the very repetition we have deceived ourselves into believing it. *It is never the supremely busy men who have no time.* So compact and systematic is the regulation of their day that whenever you make a demand on them, they seem to find additional corners to offer for unselfish service. I confess as a minister, that the men to whom I most hopefully look for additional service are the busiest men."

The problem is not that of needing more time, but of making better use of the time we have. Let us face the fact squarely that each of us has as much time as anyone else in the world. The president of the United States of America has twenty-four hours to his day, and so have we. Others may have more ability, influence, or money than we, but they have no more time.

As in the parable of the pounds (Luke 19:12-27), each servant was entrusted with the same amount of money, so we have each been granted the same amount of time. But few use it so wisely as to produce a tenfold return. It is true that not all have the same capacity; but that fact, too, is recognized in the parable. The servant who had less capacity but showed equal faithfulness received the same reward. Although we cannot be held responsible for our capacity, we are responsible for the strategic employment of our time.

When Paul urged the Ephesian Christians to "redeem the time," he was indicating that in a sense time becomes ours by purchase. There is a price to be paid for its highest employment. We exchange time in the market of life for certain occupations and activities that may be either worthy or unworthy, productive or unproductive. Weymouth renders the sentence thus: "Buy up the opportunities," for time is opportunity, and herein lies the importance of a carefully planned life. "If we progress in the economy of time, we are learning to live. If we fail here, we fail everywhere."

Time can be lost, but it can never be retrieved. It cannot be hoarded; it must be spent. Nor can it be postponed. If it is not used productively, it is irretrievably lost, as these lines that were engraved on a sundial assert:

> The shadow of my finger cast
> Divides the future from the past;
> Before it stands the unborn hour
> In darkness and beyond thy power;
> Behind its unreturning line
> The vanished hour, no longer thine;
> One hour alone is in thy hands,
> The *now* on which the shadow stands.
>
> AUTHOR UNKNOWN

In the face of that sobering fact, the leader must be meticulously careful in his selection of priorities. Comparative values of opportunities and responsibilities must be sedulously weighed. He cannot afford to squander time on that which is of only secondary importance while primary things are screaming out for attention. His day should therefore be carefully planned. If it is his ambition to excel, there must be selection and rejection, then concentration on the things of paramount importance. It is a salutary and revealing exercise to keep a faithful record of how each hour is spent in a normal week and then to analyze it in the light of scriptural priorities. The result may well be startling, even shocking in terms of spiritual values. One undoubted result would be to convince the experimenter that he has much more time than he is productively using.

After making a generous allowance of eight hours a day for sleep and rest—and few really need more than that—three hours a day for meals and social intercourse, ten hours a day for work and travel on five days, there still remain no fewer than thirty-five hours unaccounted for in each week. What happens to them? How are the extra two days in the week invested? The whole of man's contribution to the kingdom of God might well turn upon how those crucial hours are employed. They will determine whether his life will be commonplace or extraordinary.

That intrepid missionary Mary Slessor, later to become known as "The White Queen of Okoyong," was the daughter of a drunkard. She commenced working in a factory in Dundee at the age of eleven, working from six in the morning until six at night. Yet that grueling program did not prevent her from educating herself for her notable career.

David Livingstone used to work in a cotton mill in his native Dumbarton from six in the morning until eight at night. He commenced work when he was ten. He could surely have been excused if he had pleaded that he had no time for study. But so purposefully did he utilize his "leisure" hours that he mastered Latin and could read Horace and Virgil with ease before he was sixteen. By the time he was twenty-seven, he had battled his way through a medical course as well as a course in theology.[1]

In the light of those achievements, and with a host of similar examples before us, we have little basis for pleading insufficient time to achieve something worthwhile in life.

As in all else, our Lord sets the perfect example of the strategic use of time. He moved through life with measured tread, never in a hurry, though always thronged and often harassed by demanding crowds. To those who came to Him for help He gave the impression that He had no more important concern than their interests. The secret of His serenity lay in His assurance that He was working according to His Father's plan for His life—a plan that embraced every hour and made provision for every contingency. His calendar had been arranged, and through communion with His father He received each day both the words He was to say and the works He was to do. "The words that I say to you I do not speak on My own initiative, but the Father abiding in Me does His works" (John 14:10).

Christ's overriding concern was to fulfill the work committed to Him within the allotted hours. He moved in the consciousness that there was a divine timing for the events of His life. (See John 7:6; 12:23, 27; 13:1; 17:1.) Not even His loved mother was allowed to interfere with His divinely planned timetable. "What do I have to do with you? My hour has not yet come," were His salutary words (John 2:4).

Even the strong drawings of His affection for Martha and Mary and the possibility of misunderstanding could not induce Him to advance His schedule by two days (John 11:6, 9). As He reviewed His life on earth at its close, with unself-conscious complacency He claimed: "[I have] accomplished the work which thou hast given Me to do" (John 17:4). And He finished that work without any part's having been spoiled through undue haste or imperfectly completed through lack of time. He found the twenty-four hours of the day sufficient time to complete the whole will of God.

That is reflected in His corrective words to His disciples: "Are there not twelve hours in the day?" His question suggested His settled confidence in His Father's plan and His assurance of the ability to finish His work in the allotted span. Dr. J. Stuart Holden saw in our Lord's words the implications of the shortness of time and yet the sufficiency of time. There were only twelve hours in the day, but there were fully twelve hours in the day.[2] Was it not that consciousness that accounted for the selective power of the Lord? He spent His time doing things that mattered. No time was wasted on things that were not vital. The strength of moral character is derived and conserved by the refusing of the unimportant.

We could, however, become panic-stricken if we forget the number of hours in the day. We have a full twelve hours in which to learn life's lessons and to fulfill life's duties. Our Lord assures us that that will be sufficient.

No trifling in this life of mine;
Not this the path the blessed Master trod;
But every hour and power employed
Always and all for God.

Author Unknown

Viewed in the light of this overheated and over-pressured age, it is a striking fact that in the gospels there is no indication of interruptions disturbing the serenity of the Son of God. Few things are more apt to produce agitation and tension in a busy life than unexpected and unwelcome interruptions. To Him there were no such things as interruptions in His God-planned life. Those had been foreseen in His Father's planning, and He could therefore afford to be undisturbed by them. True, at times there was "no leisure so much as to eat," but there would always be time for Him to accomplish all God intended Him to do. Often the pressures that come upon the spiritual leader are the result of his having assumed responsibilities not assigned to him by God and therefore for which he cannot expect God to give the extra strength required.

One busy man told how he mastered the problem of interruptions. "Up to some years ago," he testified, "I was always annoyed by interruptions, which was really a form of selfishness on my part. People used to walk in and say, 'Well, I just had two hours to kill here in between trains, and I thought I would come and see you.' That used to bother me. Then the Lord convinced me that God sends people our way. He sent Philip to the Ethopian eunuch. He sent Barnabas to look up Saul of Tarsus. The same applies today; God sends people our way.

"So when someone comes in, I say, 'The Lord must have brought you here. Let us find out why He sent you. Let us have prayer about it.' Well, this does two things. It puts the interview on a different level because God is brought into it. Also it generally shortens the interview. If a person knows that you are looking for a reason why he is there under God, if he doesn't have one, he soon leaves for greener pastures. So take interruptions from the Lord. Then they belong in your schedule, because God was simply rearranging your daily pattern to suit Him." To the alert Christian, interruptions are only divinely interjected opportunities.

That all fits into Paul's affirmation that God has a plan for every life, that we each have been "created . . . for good works, which God prepared beforehand, that we should walk in them" (Eph. 2:10). Through daily prayer and communion, the leader must discover the details of that plan and arrange his work accordingly. Each half hour should carry its own quota of usefulness.

Some large companies require young executives to submit their plans for the coming week to their superiors by Friday evening, so important do they conceive careful planning of time to be. John Wesley and F. B. Meyer, men who achieved an incredible amount of work and exercised vast influence throughout the world, used to divide their lives into periods of five minutes and endeavored to make each period constructive.[3] Few of us could or would achieve that, but all could benefit greatly by some similar, if less ambitious, discipline. It is incredible how much reading can be crowded into the odd minutes that might otherwise be wasted. If that is questioned, let the reader experiment with the odd minutes of the coming week.

A concrete example of the way in which Dr. F. B. Meyer redeemed the time, bought up the opportunities, is recorded in his biography. "If he had a long railway journey before him, he would settle himself in his corner of the railway carriage, open his dispatch case which was fitted up as a sort of stationery cabinet, and set to work on some abstruse article, quite oblivious of his surroundings. Often at protracted conventions, and even in committee meetings, when the proceedings did not demand his undivided attention, he would unobtrusively open his case and proceed to answer letters." Another man who was a miser with time was Dr. W. E. Sangster. His son wrote of him:

> Time was never wasted. The difference between one minute and two was of considerable consequence to him. He would appear from his study. "My boy, you're not doing anything. I have exactly twenty-two minutes. We'll go for a walk. We can walk right round the common in that time." He then hurtled out of the house at tremendous speed and I normally had to run to catch him up. He would then discourse on

current affairs (five minutes), Surrey's prospects
in the county championship (two minutes), the
necessity for revival (five minutes), the reality
of the Loch Ness Monster (two minutes), and
the sanctity of William Romaine (three minutes). By that time we would be home again.[4]

Few things tend to bring a conscientious leader
into bondage more than the use of his time, and a
balanced view of the matter must be arrived at. If
he does not find a satisfactory answer, he will work
under unnecessary strain. Even after he has done
everything in his power to fulfill his obligations, there
will still remain vast areas of unmet need. Every
call for help is by no means necessarily a call from
God, for every such call cannot be responded to. If
he sincerely plans his day in the Lord's presence and
carries out that plan to the best of his ability, he can
and must leave it there. His responsibility extends
only to those matters that lie within his control. The
rest he can trustfully commit to his loving and competent heavenly Father.

Procrastination, the thief of time, is one of the
devil's most potent weapons in defrauding man of his
eternal heritage. It is a habit that is absolutely fatal
to effective spiritual leadership. Its subtlety and power lie in the fact that it corresponds so well to our
natural inclinations and innate reluctance to make important decisions. Making decisions and carrying
them through always involves considerable moral
effort. But instead of making that effort easier, the
passage of time has the reverse effect. The decision

will be even more difficult to make tomorrow—and, indeed, circumstances may have so changed that it will be too late for advantageous decision. The nettle will never grow more easy to grasp than it is now.

Do it now is a principle of action that has led many a man to worldly success, and it is no less relevant in the realm of the spiritual. A most helpful method of overcoming a built-in tendency to procrastinate is to set deadlines for oneself for reading a book, writing a difficult letter or article, doing a task, and then steadfastly refusing to overrun them.

A lifelong reader, who was also busier than most, was constantly asked by his friends, "How do you get time for it?" He always replied, "I don't get time for it; I take it."[5]

NOTES

1. *The Christian,* 29 April 1966, p. 10.
2. J. Stuart Holden, *The Gospel of the Second Chance* (London: Marshall Brothers, 1912), p. 188.
3. W. Y. Fullerton, *F. B. Meyer* (London: Marshall, Morgan & Scott, n.d.), p. 70.
4. Paul E. Sangster, *Doctor Sangster* (London: Epworth, 1962), p. 314.
5. *The Sunday School Times,* 22 November 1913, p. 713.

13

THE LEADER AND HIS READING

When you come, bring . . . the books, especially the parchments.

2 TIMOTHY 4:13

Reading maketh a full man; speaking, a ready man; writing, an exact man.

BACON

Paul's counsel to Timothy, "Give heed to reading," doubtless had reference to the public reading of the Old Testament Scriptures. His injunction is nevertheless most appropriate for other areas of reading as well. The books that Paul desired Timothy to bring to him were most probably a few choice works —Jewish history books, exegetical and explanatory of the Law and the Prophets, and perhaps some of the heathen poets from which he quoted in his sermons and letters. He wished to spend his last weeks or months to the highest profit in studying his precious books—a student to the end.

There is a parallel story told of William Tyndale during his imprisonment and shortly before his martyrdom in 1536. He wrote to the governor-in-chief asking that some of his goods might be sent:

> a warmer cap, a candle, a piece of cloth to patch my leggings . . . But above all, I beseech and entreat your clemency to be urgent with the Procureur that he may kindly permit me to have my Hebrew Bible, Hebrew Grammar and Hebrew Dictionary, that I may spend time with that in study.

Both Paul and Tyndale devoted the days before martyrdom to the study of the parchments.

In this chapter it is assumed that the main preoccupation and paramount interest of the spiritual leader will be through diligent study and the illumination of the Holy Spirit to attain a mastery of the Word of God. It is his supplementary reading, however, that is our present concern.

The man who desires to grow spiritually and intellectually will be constantly at his books. The lawyer who desires to succeed in his profession must keep abreast of important cases and changes in the law. The medical practitioner must follow the constantly changing discoveries in his field. Even so the spiritual leader must master God's Word and its principles and know as well what is going on in the minds of those who look to him for guidance. To achieve those ends, he must, hand in hand with his personal contacts, engage in a course of selective reading. Today, the practice of reading solid and rewarding spiritual and classical literature is seriously on the wane. In an age in which people have more leisure than ever before in the history of the world, many claim that they have no time to read. That excuse is never valid with a spiritual leader.

John Wesley had a passion for reading, and most of it was done on horseback. He rode sometimes ninety and often fifty miles in a day. He read deeply on a wide range of subjects. It was his habit to travel with a volume of science or history or medicine propped on the pommel of his saddle, and in that way he got through thousands of volumes. After his Greek New Testament, three great books took complete possession of Wesley's mind and heart during his Oxford days. "It was about this time that he began the earnest study of the *Imitation of Christ, Holy Living and Dying* and *The Serious Call*. Those three books became very much his spiritual guides."[1] He told the younger ministers of the Wesleyan societies either to read or get out of the ministry!

The determination to spend a minimum of half an hour a day in reading worthwhile books that provide food for the soul and further mental and spiritual development will prove richly rewarding to those who have been inclined to limit their reading to predigested or superficial books.

In a very perceptive series of articles in *The Alliance Weekly* on the subject "The Use and Abuse of Books," Dr. A. W. Tozer had some arresting things to say:

Why does today's Christian find the reading of great books always beyond him? Certainly intellectual powers do not wane from one generation to another. We are as smart as our fathers, and any thought they could entertain we can entertain if we are sufficiently interested to make the effort. The major cause of the decline in the quality of current Christian literature is not intellectual but spiritual. To enjoy a great religious book requires a degree of consecration to God and detachment from the world that few modern Christians have. The early Christian Fathers, the Mystics, the Puritans, are not hard to understand, but they inhabit the highlands where the air is crisp and rarefied, and none but the God-enamoured can come. . . . One reason why people are unable to understand great Christian classics is that they are trying to understand without any intention of obeying them.[2]

WHY READ?

"Read to refill the wells of inspiration," was the advice of Harold J. Ockenga, who took a suitcase full of books on his honeymoon![3]

Bacon's famous rule for reading was: "Read, not to contradict or confute, nor to believe and take for granted, nor to find talk and discourse, but to weigh and consider. Some books are to be tested, others to be swallowed, and some few to be chewed and digested."[4]

Another writer gave as his opinion that if we read

because we want to stock our minds like a warehouse or because we like feeling superior or being thought intellectual, then it is useless or worse than useless.

The spiritual leader should read for *spiritual quickening* and profit, and that will strongly influence his selection of books for reading. There are some authors whose writings challenge heart and conscience and hold us to the highest. The reading that provides impulse and inspiration is to be cherished.

The spiritual leader should read with a view to *mental stimulation* and should have on hand, among others, some book that involves him in mental gymnastics—something that calls for his utmost mental powers and stimulates fresh thoughts and ideas.

He should read for *cultivation of style* in his preaching and teaching and writing. For that, nothing can equal the writing of those masters who enlarge our vocabularies, teach us to think, and instruct us in the art of incisive and compelling speech. In speaking of the masters, Dr. Tozer recommended "John Bunyan for simplicity, Joseph Addison for clarity and elegance, John Milton for nobility and consistent elevation of thought, Charles Dickens for sprightliness, and Francis Bacon for conciseness and dignity."[5] Bacon himself claimed that "histories make men wise; poets, witty; the mathematics, subtle; natural philosophy, deep; moral, grave; logic and rhetoric, able to contend."

The leader should read, too, with a view to the *acquiring of information*. Never was there such a vast range of information within the reach of every reader as today. It is mainly through reading that information is assimilated. He should read, therefore, to keep abreast of his age, and should be reasonably well informed in his own field.

He should read in order to have *fellowship with great minds*. It is possible to hold communion with the greatest and godliest of men of all ages through the medium of their writings.

The power for good of even one book is impossible to estimate. In his *Curiosities of Literature,* Benjamin Disraeli entitles one chapter "The Man of One Book," and gives a number of instances of the remarkable influence of a solitary work. In reading the biographies of a number of great Christians whom God used in a unique way in the past century, the author noticed time and again that the same book had induced a crisis in their lives and produced a revolution in their ministry. The book was *Lectures on Revivals of Religion* by Charles G. Finney.

On the other hand, who can measure the power for evil of a single book such as Hitler's *Mein Kampf?* Who can gauge the spiritual havoc wrought by Bishop Robinson's *Honest to God?*

WHAT TO READ

If it is true that a man is known by the company he keeps, it is no less true that his character is reflected in the books he reads, for they are the outward expression of his inner hungers and aspirations. The vast number of books, both secular and religious, that are pouring from the presses today makes discrimination in reading imperative. We can afford to read only the best and what will be most helpful to us in the fulfillment of our mission. In other words, our reading should be regulated largely by what we are and what we do or intend to do.

An old writer who adopted the pseudonym Cladius Clear suggested that a booklover could divide his books as he would people. A few he would term "lovers," and they would be the books he would take with him if he were exiled. Others, and more than in the first class, he would call "friends." The majority he would designate "acquaintances," books with which he was on nodding terms and to which he occasionally referred.[6]

Matthew Arnold gave the opinion that the best of literature was to be found within the covers of five hundred books. Daniel Webster preferred to master a few books rather than to read indiscriminately. It was his contention that reading a few great writers who have built up the permanent literature of the English language, well mastered, was better than skimming a multitude of ephemeral works. He maintained it was to them we should turn for a real knowledge of the human heart, its aspirations and tragedies, hopes and disappointments. Hobbes, the English philosopher, once said, "If I had read as many books as other people, I would know as little."

Samuel Brengle had this to say about his preferences in poetry:

> I like the poets whose writings reveal great moral character and passion—such as Tenny-

son's and some of Browning's. The works of others have light, but I prefer flame to just light. Shakespeare? A mind as clear as a sunbeam—but passionless, light without heat. Shelley? Keats? There's a sense in which they were perfect poets. But they don't move me. Beautiful—but wordmongers. There's an infinite difference between the beauty of holiness and the holiness of beauty. One leads to the highest, loftiest, most Godlike character; the other often—too often—leads to an orgy of sensation.[7]

Sir W. Robertson Nicoll, for many years editor of *The British Weekly,* found biography the most attractive form of general reading because biography transmits personality. One cannot read the lives of great and consecrated men and women without having inspiration kindled and aspiration aroused. The "lives of great men still remind us that we may make our lives sublime." Who can gauge the inspiration to the cause of missions of great biographies like those of William Carey, Adoniram Judson, Hudson Taylor, Charles Studd, or Albert Simpson?

Joseph W. Kemp, who exercised a wide preaching and teaching ministry, made a point of always keeping a good biography on hand. Ransome W. Cooper maintains, "The reading of good biography forms an important part of a Christian's education. It provides him with numberless illustrations for use in his own service. He learns to assess the true worth of character, to glimpse a work goal for his own life, to decide how best to attain it, what self-denial is needed to curb unworthy aspirations; and all the time he learns how God breaks into the dedicated life to bring about His own purposes."

What satisfies those who follow him should not satisfy the leader, in the matter of the books he reads. Nor should he be content to read only those books that can be easily read or books along the line of his own speciality.

Muriel Ormrod counseled:

> It is better that we should always tackle something a bit beyond us. "We should always aim to read something different—not only the writers with whom we agree, but those with whom we are ready to do battle. And let us not condemn them out of hand because they do not agree with us; their point of view challenges us to examine the truth and to test their views against Scripture. And let us not comment on nor criticize writers of whom we have heard only second-hand, or third-hand, without troubling to read their works for ourselves. . . . Don't be afraid of new ideas—and don't be carried away with them either.[8]

*   *   *   *

A little learning is a dangerous thing;
Drink deep, or taste not the Pierian Spring;
There shallow draughts intoxicate the brain,
And drinking largely sobers us again.

ALEXANDER POPE

The leader, then, should immerse himself in books that will further equip him for a higher quality of service and leadership in the kingdom of God.

HOW TO READ

Reading, in one of its senses, is defined as learning from written or printed matter; and that involves not only scanning the reading symbols but meditating on the thoughts they express. "It is easy to read. It is much more difficult to secure effectually the fruit of reading in the mind. And yet, to what profit is our reading if it does not achieve this end?"

When Southey, the poet, was telling an old Quaker lady how he learned Portuguese grammar while he washed, and something else while he dressed, and how he gleaned in another field while he breakfasted, and so on, filling his day utterly, she said quietly, "And when does thee think?" It is possible to read without thinking, but we cannot profit from what we read unless we think. Charles H. Spurgeon counseled his students:

> Master those books you have. Read them thoroughly. Bathe in them until they saturate you. Read and reread them, masticate them and digest them. Let them go into your very self. Peruse a good book several times and make notes and analyses of it. A student will find that his mental constitution is more affected by one book thoroughly mastered than by twenty books he has merely skimmed. Little learning and much pride come of hasty reading. Some men

> are disabled from thinking by their putting medi-
> tation away for the sake of much reading. In
> reading let your motto be "much, not many."[9]

The following rules for reading have been found to make reading more meaningful and of more lasting benefit:

• Read little that is to be immediately forgotten since that only helps to form the habit of forgetting. Exercise the same discrimination in choosing books as in choosing friends.

• Read with pencil and notebook in hand. Unless the memory is unusually vigorous and retentive, much reading will be a waste of time. Develop a system of note-taking, and it will be astonishing to discover how greatly that practice aids the memory.

• Have a "commonplace book," as it used to be called, a book in which to put what is striking, inter-esting, and worthy of permanent record. One's own comments and criticisms may be added. In that way an irreplaceable accumulation of material will be pre-served and indexed for future use.

• Verify as far as possible historical, scientific, and other data, and let no word slip past until its mean-ing is understood.

• Let reading be varied, because the mind so easily runs into ruts. Variety is as restful to the mind as to the body.

• Reading should be correlated where possible—history with poetry, biography with historical novels; that is, when reading the history of the American Civil

War, read the biographies of Lincoln and Grant and the poems written by Walt Whitman on Abraham Lincoln.

Canon Yates gives advice on reading that would be most helpful to those able to follow it. To some, however, the pressures of the space age might make it seem a counsel of perfection.

He suggests that every solid book requires three readings. The first reading should be rapid and continuous. The subconscious mind will then go to work on it and link it up with what you already know on the subject. Then take time to think what contribution it has made to your knowledge. The second reading should be careful, slow and detailed, as you think out each new point and make notes for later use. After an interval, the third reading should be fairly rapid and continuous, and a brief analysis should be written in the back of the book, with page references to subjects and illustrations.

A minister in the little manse of Lumsden in Scotland, gathered around him no fewer than seventeen thousand volumes, among which he browsed with great delight. But of him and his books his son said, "Though he spent much time and pains on his sermons, he did not cut a channel between them and his reading."[10]

Here is a danger of which the leader must be aware. Ideally a book is a channel through which ideas can flow from one mind to another. The Lumsden minister did not fail to cut a channel linking his reading and his own spiritual life, but his congregation did not derive the benefit it should have enjoyed as a result of his wide reading. It is for the leader to cut a channel between what he reads and what he says or writes, so that others may reap its benefits to the full.

A country minister in Australia, who is known to the author, is a great book lover. Early in his ministry he decided that he would aim at developing a biblically and theologically literate congregation. He succeeded in conveying to members of his church his own love of books and introduced them gradually to spiritual works of increasing weight and depth. The result is that in that district a number of farmers have accumulated libraries that would be no disgrace to a minister of the gospel. If they aimed at it, many more ministers could communicate their appreciation of spiritual books to their congregations by guiding them in a course of selected reading.

NOTES

1. Alexander Whyte, *Thirteen Appreciations* (London: Oliphants, 1913), p. 364.
2. A. W. Tozer, "The Use and Abuse of Books," 22 February 1956, p. 2.
3. Harold J. Ockenga, in *Christianity Today*, 4 March 1966, p. 36.
4. Francis Bacon, in *The Alliance Weekly*, 14 March 1956, p. 2.
5. A. W. Tozer, in *The Sunday School Times*, 22 November 1913, p. 713.
6. Cladius Clear, in *The Life of Faith*, 26 November 1913, p. 1443.
7. C. W. Hall, *Samuel Logan Brengle* (New York: Salvation Army, 1933), p. 269.
8. Muriel Ormrod, *The Reaper*, August 1965, p. 229
9. Helmut Thielecke, *Encounter with Spurgeon* (Philadelphia: Fortress, 1963), p. 197.
10. *Sunday School Times*, 22 November 1913, p. 715.

14

IMPROVING LEADERSHIP POTENTIAL

If you are a leader, exert yourself to lead.
Romans 12:8, *NEB*

Every Christian is under obligation to be the best he can be for God. If his leadership potential can be improved, he must do it. Because none of us knows what the future holds, we should prepare ourselves in every way possible for opportunities of service that may open up.

Not every Christian is called to or qualified for a position of major leadership, but all are leaders to the extent that they influence others. All of us can, if we will, increase our leadership potential.

The first step to achieve that end is to discover and correct weaknesses in that area and to cultivate our strengths. Various reasons have been advanced to explain the prevalence of mediocre leadership in Christian work, and a perusal of the following suggested causes may disclose areas that could be improved and strengthened.

Is it that we lack a clearly defined goal that will stretch and stimulate us, challenge faith, and unify life's activities? Are we timid in faith, hesitant to take steps in the interests of the kingdom that will involve a risk? Do we usually prefer to play safe? Are we effervescent with zeal or tepid in enthusiasm. It is the enthusiastic leader who creates enthusiastic followers.

Are we reluctant to grasp the nettle of the difficult situation and deal courageously with it? Or do we procrastinate, in the vain hope that the problem will just go away? It seldom does. It is the mediocre leader who postpones difficult decisions, interviews, or letters. Delay solves nothing, but usually exacerbates the problem. Do we sacrifice depth for area, and, by spreading ourselves too thinly, achieve only superficial results?

EXERT YOURSELF TO LEAD

Romans 12 holds much for the leader. It begins in verse 1 with the aorist tense of consecration: "Present your bodies [once and for all] a living and holy sacrifice." That blanket injunction is followed by thirty-six present tenses that specify the results that should flow from that initial act. Two of those are specially relevant to our theme.

The first is, "If you are a leader, *exert yourself to lead,*" or, "If called upon to supply leadership, *do it with zeal*" (v. 8, Barclay, italics added). Here is a summons to undertake our leadership responsibilities with intensity and zeal. There is no room for laziness or self-indulgence. We must positively exert ourselves, put everything we have into it. Are we doing that?

Is there *intensity* in our leadership? It was characteristic of our Master. When His disciples saw Him ablaze with sinless anger and righteous indignation at the desecration of His Father's house, disturbing the rhythm of the centuries, they "remembered that it was written, 'Zeal for Thy house will consume Me' " (John 2:17). So intense was the zeal with which He pursued His divinely-given task, that His friends said, "He has lost His senses," whereas his enemies charged, "You have a demon" (Mark 3:21; John 7:20).

Similar intensity and zeal marked the service of the apostle Paul at every stage of his life. Adolph Deissman wrote of him, "The lightning of the Damascus road found plenty of inflammable material in the soul of the young persecutor. We see the flames shoot up, and we feel the glow then kindled lost none of its brightness in Paul the aged." We should covet that continuing intensity as we grow older, but it is not automatic. The flame always tends to die down to dull embers. Fresh fuel must constantly be fed to the flame.

Before his conversion, Paul's burning but misguided zeal drove him to terrible acts of cruelty for which he never forgave himself. "I persecuted the church of God," he mourned. But that same zeal, purged by the Holy Spirit, carried over into his new life and led to incredible achievements in the interests of the church he had sought to destroy.

Because he was constantly full of the Spirit, his

mind was aflame with the truth of God, his heart aglow with the love of God, and his will ablaze with a passion for the glory of God. No wonder people were willing to follow him to the death. He constantly exerted himself to lead. He did it with intensity and zeal, and that spirit rubbed off on those who were associated with him in service.

KEPT AT BOILING POINT

The second present tense we will note in Romans 12 is in verse 11: "Never flag in zeal, *be aglow with the Spirit,* serve the Lord" (RSV, italics added), or, "Not slothful in business, *kept at boiling point by the Holy Spirit,* doing bondservice for the Master" (Harrington C. Lees, italics added).

It is one thing to discover areas of weakness, but quite another to remedy them. In this verse we are given the *dynamic for consistent zealous service:* "Kept at boiling point by the Holy Spirit." For most in leadership positions, it is not too difficult to come to boiling point on special occasions. Most have known times of spiritual exaltation, of the burning heart, of special nearness to God and more than ordinary fruitfulness in service, but the problem is, how to stay there! This verse holds out the alluring possibility of being kept "aglow with the Spirit." It implies that there is no necessity for us to go "off the boil," for the Holy Spirit is the great central furnace in our lives.

Bunyan's Christian discovered the secret when he visited the Interpreter's house. He was at a loss to see the flames leaping higher when someone was pouring water on them. He understood when he saw someone in the rear pouring on oil. Have we learned that secret?

In His classic dissertation on prayer, Jesus made a pregnant promise: "If you then, being evil, know how to give good gifts to your children, how much more shall your heavenly Father give the Holy Spirit to those who ask Him?" (Luke 11:13). That verse holds a problem of interpretation for those who rightly believe that on trusting Christ for salvation, one receives the Holy Spirit. "If anyone does not have the Spirit of Christ, he does not belong to Him" (Rom. 8:9).

But if every believer has the Holy Spirit, what is the point of asking for Him? The answer lies in the grammar of the verse. In our English New Testament, the phrase "the Holy Spirit" occurs eighty-eight times. In the Greek, however, in only fifty-four of those instances is the definite article, "the," found. In the remaining thirty-four occurrences, no definite article is found—it is simply "Holy Spirit." That is the case in Luke 11:13. It was H. B. Swete's contention that where there is the definite article, the reference is to *the Holy Spirit as a Person*. But where there is no definite article, the reference is not to the Person, but to *the operations of the Holy Spirit*.

That opens up a wide vista of possibility. Jesus was assuring the disciples that they could ask for whatever operation of the Spirit they needed to fulfill their service to the Body of Christ, and the Father would bestow it. Are we availing ourselves of that amazing provision? Is our need love, or power, or courage, or wisdom? *"How much more* shall your heavenly Father give [that operation of] the Holy Spirit to those who ask Him" (italics added). It was in that very connection that Jesus had said to them, "Ask, and it shall be given to you" (Luke 11:9).

IMPROVING LEADERSHIP

Hudson Taylor, founder of the China Inland Mission, was a simple yet very astute man. He had the gift of saying tremendously significant things in a deceptively simple way. One of such statements enshrined his philosophy of the leader's responsibility and his prescription for improving his performance. A careful study of his statement and an application of its principles would greatly improve leadership potential.

In a letter written from Hong Kong in 1879 to Mr. B. Broomhall, then secretary of the mission, Mr. Taylor said:

The all-important thing to do is to

1. Improve the character of the work
2. Deepen the piety, devotion and success of the workers
3. Remove stones of stumbling, if possible
4. Oil the wheels where they stick
5. Amend whatever is defective
6. Supplement, as far as may be, what is lacking.

This is no easy matter where suitable men are
wanting, or only in the course of formation. That
I may be used of God, at least in some measure,
to bring this to pass is my hope.

That simple statement reveals an acute insight into
the responsibilities of leadership. An analysis high-
lights six important areas to be cared for.

• *Administration.* "To improve the character of the
work." It is for the leader to discover which depart-
ments of the operation are functioning below the opti-
mum level and to remedy the defect. It may involve
drawing up new or better job descriptions, or ensuring
that the lines of communication are clear.

• *Spiritual Tone.* "To deepen the piety, devotion
and success of the worker." The tone of a church,
mission, or other group will largely be a reflection of
that of its leaders. Water rises no higher than its
source. The spiritual health of the leadership group
should therefore be the paramount concern of those
in top positions. Job satisfaction is also important.
If leaders can show their colleagues the way to experience greater success, their sense of fulfillment will
be reflected in the quality of their work.

• *Group Morale.* "To remove stones of stumbling."
Morale is the attitude that leads to people working together as a team with a minimum of friction. When
matters that call for attention are neglected and allowed to drift, morale drops and performance is affected. If the stumbling block is a factor that can be
remedied, it should be done at once. If it is a person,
the delinquent should be dealt with as soon as the facts

are clear, and let the chips fall. Of course the person or group involved should be treated with consideration and love, but the work of God should not be sacrificed for the sake of keeping peace.

• *Personal Relationships.* "To oil the wheels where they stick." The importance of maintaining warm relationships with personnel cannot be overemphasized. People are more important than administration. Some love administration, others love people. It is the latter who are the leaders. In handling personnel, the oil can is much more effective than the acid bottle.

• *Problem Solving.* "To amend what is defective." One of the main functions of leadership is to discover or provide solutions to intractable problems in the operation. It is easy to create problems but difficult to solve them. The leader must face the problem realistically and follow it through until a satisfactory solution is reached.

• *Creative Planning.* "To supplement what is lacking." It is much easier to criticize plans submitted than to create more satisfactory ones. The leader must not only see clearly the goal that is to be reached, but also plan imaginative strategy and tactics by which it can be attained. This is an area in which there is a perennial short supply.

One more way in which leadership potential can be improved is to refuse to submit to what has been termed "leadership from the rear." True leadership comes from the top down, not from the bottom up. It was leadership from the rear that led Israel back into the wilderness.

Many churches and organizations are stalemated because the leaders, instead of giving a strong lead, submit to a form of blackmail from the rear. No small dissident or reactionary element should be allowed to determine the policy of a group, when the consensus of the spiritual leaders is in the opposite direction.

15

THE COST OF LEADERSHIP

Are you able to drink the cup that I drink, or to be baptized with the baptism with which I am baptized?

MARK 10:38

No one need aspire to leadership in the work of God who is not prepared to pay a price greater than his contemporaries and colleagues are willing to pay. True leadership always exacts a heavy toll on the whole man, and the more effective the leadership is, the higher the price to be paid.

Quinton Hogg, founder of the London Polytechnic Institute, devoted a great fortune to the enterprise. Asked how much it had cost to build up such a great institution, Hogg replied: "Not very much, simply one man's life blood."[1] That is the cost of every great achievement, and it is not paid in a lump sum. It is bought on the time-payment plan, a further installment each new day. Fresh drafts are constantly being made, and when the payment ceases, the leadership wanes. That fact was taught by the Lord when He indicated that we could not save others and save ourselves at the same time.

Samuel Brengle wrote:

> Spiritual power is the outpouring of spiritual life, and like all life, from that of the moss and lichen on the wall to that of the archangel before the throne, is from God. Therefore those who aspire to leadership must pay the price, and seek it from God.[2]

SELF-SACRIFICE

Self-sacrifice is part of the price that must be paid daily. A cross stands in the way of spiritual leadership, a cross upon which the leader must consent to be impaled. Heaven's demands are absolute. "He laid down his life for us; and we ought to lay down our lives for the brethren" (1 John 3:16). The degree to which we allow the cross of Christ to work in us will be the measure in which the resurrection life of Christ can be manifested through us. "Death worketh in me, but life in you." To evade the cross is to forfeit leadership.

"Whoever wishes to be first among you shall be slave of all. For even the Son of Man did not come to be served, but to serve, and to *give His life* a ransom for many" (Mark 10:44-45, italics added). Each of the heroes of faith immortalized in Hebrews 11 was called to sacrifice as well as to service. Willingness to renounce personal preferences, to sacrifice legitimate and natural desires for the sake of His kingdom, will characterize those marked out by God for positions of influence in His work. Bruce Barton quotes a pertinent advertisement at a service station: "We will crawl under your car oftener and get ourselves dirtier than any of our competitors." Is that not the service station you would patronize?

Dr. Samuel M. Zwemer recalls the striking fact that the only thing Jesus took pains to show after His resurrection was His scars.[3] His disciples recoginzed neither Him nor His message on the Emmaus road. Not until He broke the bread and they possibly saw the scars were their sensibilities aroused. When He stood in the midst of His demoralized disciples in the upper room after the resurrection, "He showed them both His hands and His side."

Scars are the authentic marks of faithful discipleship and true spiritual leadership. It was said of one leader, "He belonged to that class of early martyrs whose passionate soul made an early holocaust of the physical man."[4] Nothing moves people more than the print of the nails and the mark of the spear. Those are tests of sincerity that no one can challenge, as Paul well knew. "From now on let no one cause trouble for me, for I bear on my body the brand-marks of Jesus" (Gal. 6:17).

> Hast thou no scar?
> No hidden scar on foot, or side, or hand?
> I hear thee sung as mighty in the land,
> I hear them hail thy bright ascendant star:
> Hast thou no scar?

Hast thou no wound?
Yet, I was wounded by the archers, spent.
Leaned me against the tree to die, and rent
By ravening beasts that compassed me, I
    swooned:
Hast thou no wound?

No wound? No scar?
Yes, as the master shall the servant be,
And pierced are the feet that follow Me;
But thine are whole. Can he have followed
    far
Who has no wound? No scar?

                      AMY WILSON CARMICHAEL*

That Paul was willing to pay the price and carried
the authentic scars incidental to leadership is attested
by an autobiographical paragraph in one of his letters.

On every hand hard-pressed am I—yet not
    crushed!
In desperate plight am I—yet not in despair!
Close followed by pursuers—yet not abandoned
    by Him!
Beaten to earth—yet never destroyed!
Evermore bearing about in my body
The imminence of such a death as Jesus died,
So that the life, too, of Jesus might be shown
    forth
    In this body of mine
    Always, always while I yet live

*Used by permission of Christian Literature Crusade, Fort
Washington, Pa.

Am I being handed over to death's doom
　　For Jesus' sake!
So that in this mortal flesh of mine, may be
　　Shown forth also
The very life of Jesus

　　　　　　　　2 CORINTHIANS 4:8-11 (Way)

LONELINESS

It was Nietzsche's contention that life always gets harder toward the summit—the cold increases, the responsibility increases.

From its very nature, the lot of the leader must be a lonely one. He must always be ahead of his followers. Though he be the friendliest of men, there are areas of life in which he must be prepared to tread a lonely path. That fact dawned painfully on Dixon E. Hoste when Hudson Taylor laid down the direction of the China Inland Mission and appointed Hoste his successor. After the interview during which the appointment was made, the new leader, sensible of the weight of responsibility that now was his, said, "And now I have no one, no one but God!" In his journey to the top he had left behind all his contemporaries and stood alone on the mount with his God.

Human nature craves company, and it is only natural to wish to share with others the heavy burdens of responsibility and care. It is often heartbreaking to have to make decisions of far-reaching importance that affect the lives of loved fellow workers—and to make them alone. It is one of the heaviest prices to pay, but it must be paid. Moses paid the price for his leadership—alone on the mount, and alone in the plain; the crushing loneliness of misunderstanding and criticism and impugning of motive. And times have not changed.

The prophets were the loneliest of men. Enoch walked alone in a decadent society as he proclaimed the impending judgment, but he was compensated by the presence of God. Who could have experienced the pangs of loneliness more than Jonah as he proclaimed the message of an imminent judgment, which could be averted only by immediate repentance, to a heathen city of a million souls? The loneliest preacher today is the man who has been entrusted with a prophetic message that is ahead of his times, a message that cuts across the prevailing temper of the age.

The gregarious Paul was a lonely man who experienced to the full the bitterness of misunderstanding by his contemporaries, misrepresentation by enemies, and desertion by converts and friends. How poignant is his word to Timothy: "You are aware of the fact that all who are in Asia turned away from me" (2 Tim. 1:15).

"Most of the world's great souls have been lonely," wrote A. W. Tozer. "Loneliness seems to be the price a saint must pay for his saintliness." The leader must be a man who, while welcoming the friendship and support of all who can offer it, has sufficient inner resources to stand alone, even in the face of fierce opposition, in the discharge of his responsibilities. He must be prepared to have "no one but God."

On without cheer of sister or of daughter,
   Yes, without stay of father or of son,
Lone on the land, and homeless on the water,
   Pass I in patience till my work be done.

F. W. H. MEYERS

FATIGUE

"The world is run by tired men." Although that statement may be challenged, there is more than a grain of reality in the assertion. The ever increasing demands made on a leader drain the nervous resources and wear down the most robust physique. But he knews where to go for renewal. Paul was familiar with the secret. "Therefore we do not lose heart, but though our outer man is decaying, yet our inner man is being renewed day by day" (2 Cor. 4: 15-16). The ministry of our Lord wearied him, so He rested by the well (John 4:6). When the needy woman touched the hem of His garment in faith, Jesus was aware that power, nervous force, had gone out of him (Mark 5:30). No real lasting good can be done without the outgoing of power and the expenditure of nervous energy.

The man who has absorbed the spirit of the welfare state is not of the caliber required in a leader. If he is not willing to rise earlier and stay up later than others, to work harder and study more diligently than his contempories, he will not greatly impress his generation. If he is unwilling to pay the price of fatigue for his leadership, it will always be mediocre, unless he is a man of unusual physique and resilience.

If he is wise, however, he will seize every legitimate opportunity for recuperation and recreation, or he will limit his own usefulness and ministry.

Writing to the secretary of the Church Missionary Society, Douglas M. Thornton of Egypt said:

> But I am weary! I have only written because I am too weary to be working now, and too tired to sleep . . . I am getting prematurely old, they tell me, and doctors do not give me long to live unless the strain is eased a bit. My wife is wearier than I am. She needs complete rest a while. . . . Oh, that the church at home but realized one half of the opportunities of today! Will no one hear the call? Please do your best to help us.[5]

Here were missionary leaders willing to pay the price of fatigue in order to grasp the swiftly passing opportunities of their day.

When Robert Murray McCheyne, the saintly young Scottish minister, lay dying at the age of twenty-nine, he turned to a friend who was sitting with him and said: "God gave me a message to deliver and a horse to ride. Alas, I have killed the horse and now I cannot deliver the message." There is no virtue in flogging the tired horse to death.

CRITICISM

"There is nothing else that so kills the efficiency, capability and initiative of a leader as destructive criticism. . . . Its destructive effect cannot be underestimated. It tends to hamper and undercut the efficiency of a man's thinking process. It chips away at his self-respect and undermines his confidence in his ability to cope with his responsibilities."[6]

No leader is exempt from criticism, and his humility will nowhere be seen more clearly than in the manner in which he accepts and reacts to it.

In a letter to a young minister, Fred Mitchell once wrote:

> I am glad to know that you are taking any blessing there is about the criticism brought against you by _____, in which case even his bitter attack will yield sweetness. A sentence which has been a great help to Mrs. Mitchell and myself is: "It does not matter what happens to us, but our reaction to what happens to us is of vital importance." I think you must expect more and more criticism, for with increasing responsibility this is inevitable. It causes one to walk humbly with God, and to take such action as He desires.[7]

Samuel Brengle, who was noted for his genuine holiness, had been subjected to caustic criticism. Instead of replying in kind or resorting to self-justification, he replied: "From my heart I thank you for your rebuke. I think I deserved it. Will you, my comrade, remember me in prayer?" On another occasion, a biting, censorious attack was made on his spiritual life. His answer was: "I thank you for your criticism of my life. It set me to self-examination and heart-searching and prayer, which always leads me into a deeper sense of my utter dependence on Jesus for holiness of heart, and into sweeter fellowship with Him."[8]

With such an attitude, criticism is turned from a curse into a blessing, from a liability into an asset.

REJECTION

The leader who maintains high spiritual standards may sometimes find himself following his Master on the pathway of rejection, for "he came unto his own and his own received him not." That is not always the case, but it has been the experience of many.

Dr. J. Gregory Mantle tells of a ministerial friend whose congregation persistently refused to accept his message. He wanted to lead his flock into the green pastures and beside the still waters, but they were unwilling to be led. His choir, with their ungodly practices, brought things to a head.

The position became so untenable that he invited the choir to resign. The choir not only resigned but persuaded the congregation to desist from taking any part in the singing on the following Sunday. The result was that whatever singing was done, had to be done by the minister, while the choir and congregation enjoyed his discomfiture. That state of things continued for some time and the minister was greatly dejected and perplexed at the turn events had taken.

He was at his wits' end when God spoke to him. One day he was sitting on a seat in a park when he saw part of a torn newspaper before him on the ground. The torn piece bore a message for him that exactly suited his need. It was this:

"No man is ever fully accepted until he has,
first of all, been utterly rejected."

He needed nothing more. He had been utterly rejected for Christ's sake, and his recognition of the fact was the beginning of a most fruitful ministry. Though utterly rejected by man, he had been fully accepted by God.

When, in response to the clear call of God, Dr. A. B. Simpson resigned his pastorate, he learned what it meant to be "destitute, despised, forsaken." He surrendered a salary of $5,000, a position as a leading pastor in the greatest American city, and all claim on his denomination for assistance in a yet untried work. He was in a great city with no following, no organization, no financial resources, with a large family dependent on him, and with his most intimate ministerial friends and former associates predicting failure. So completely was he misunderstood, even by those from whom he expected sympathy, that he once said he often looked down upon the paving stones in the street for the sympathy denied him elsewhere.

"The rugged path of utter rejection was trodden not only uncomplainingly, but with rejoicing. He knew that though he . . . was going through fire and water, it was the divinely appointed way to the wealthy place."[9]

And it was a wealthy place into which Dr. Simpson was brought. At his death he left behind five schools for the training of missionaries, hundreds of missionaries in sixteen lands, and a large number of congregations in the United States and Canada that exerted a spiritual influence far beyond their numerical strength.

"Often the crowd does not recognize a leader until he has gone, and then they build a monument for him with the stones they threw at him in life."[10]

PRESSURE AND PERPLEXITY

It might be thought by those who have not found themselves in a position of leadership that greater experience and a longer walk with God would result in much greater ease in discerning the will of God in perplexing situations. But the reverse is often the case. God treats the leader as a mature adult, leaving more and more to his spiritual discernment, and giving fewer sensible and tangible evidences of His guidance than in earlier years. That perplexity adds to the inevitable pressures incidental to any responsible office.

In one of his few moments of self-revelation, D. E. Hoste said to a friend:

> The pressure! It goes on from stage to stage, pressed beyond measure. . . . It changes with every period of your life. The most killing years of my life were 1904-1906, terrible! I was half-killed! One has been able to make arrangements since then. But other things develop. He eases you at one end, brings you into new things at the other.
>
> I more and more see that as we go on in the

Christian life, the Lord very often does not want to give us the sense of His presence, or the consciousness of His help. There again Mr. Hudson Taylor helped me very much. We were talking about guidance. He said how in his younger days, things used to come so clearly, so quickly to him. "But," he said, "now as I have gone on, and God has used me more and more, I seem often to be like a man going along in a fog. I do not know what to do."[11]

But when the time came to act, God always responded to His servant's trust.

COST TO OTHERS

There is often a very real cost that has to be paid by persons other than the one entrusted with leadership. Indeed, it is they who sometimes pay the heavier price. When Fred Mitchell, a valued colleague of the author, was invited to become British director of the China Inland Mission, he realized that there would be a price to pay, not only by himself but by those dearest to him.

He wrote:

My hands were already full, and I had no desire for more work. I have lived long enough, and have already had sufficient responsibility to know that it is not to be sought, for it is usually carried at a heavy price.

To one of his children he later wrote:

I have had many a sorrow of heart, and it

still remains one of my chief regrets that I have not been able to give myself to mother and you children more. The harvest is great and the labourers few, which means that there have been many calls upon me. I do not justify my negligence . . . but any sacrifice made by you for our dear Lord Jesus' sake has not been unrewarded.[12]

REACTION TO ADVERSE OPINION

Paul set a valuable pattern in this regard. It was his ambition to secure the favor of God, not of men. "For am I now seeking the favor of men, or of God? Or am I striving to please men?" (Gal. 1:10).

He was not unduly disturbed by the adverse opinion of his fellowmen. "To me it is a very small thing that I should be examined by you, or by any human court. . . . The one who examines me is the Lord" (1 Cor. 4:3-4). The world was not his judge. He could afford to sit lightly to mere human opinion, because his heart was single toward God (Col. 3:22). But indifference to human opinion can be disastrous when it is not linked to fear of God. Such independence, however, can be a valuable asset to the disciplined man whose aim is the glory of God. To Paul, the voice of man was faint because his ear was tuned to the louder voice of God's appraisal. He was fearless of man's judgment because he was conscious he stood before a higher tribunal (2 Cor. 8:21).

NOTES

1. Robert E. Speer, *Marks of a Man* (New York: Revell, 1907), p. 109.
2. Samuel Logan Brengle, *The Soul-winner's Secret* (London: Salvation Army, 1918), p. 23.
3. Samuel M. Zwemer, *It Is Hard to Be a Christian* (London: Marshalls, 1937), p. 139.
4. Lettie B. Cowman, *Charles E. Cowman* (Los Angeles: Oriental Missionary Society, 1928), p. 260.
5. W. H. T. Gairdner, *Douglas M. Thornton* (London: Hodder & Stoughton, n.d.), p. 225.
6. R. D. Abella, in *Evangelical Thrust* (Manila, n.d.).
7. Phyllis Thompson, *Climbing on Track* (London: China Inland Mission, 1954), p. 116.
8. C. W. Hall, *Samuel Logan Brengle* (New York: Salvation Army, 1933), p. 272.
9. J. Gregory Mantle, *Beyond Humiliation* (Chicago: Moody, n.d.), pp. 140-41.
10. Cowman, p. 258.
11. Phyllis Thompson, *D. E. Hoste* (London: China Inland Mission, n.d.), pp. 130-31.
12. Phyllis Thompson, *Climbing on Track,* p. 115.

16

THE RESPONSIBILITIES OF LEADERSHIP

Apart from such external things, there is the daily pressure upon me of concern for all the churches.

2 CORINTHIANS 11:28

To serve was Jesus' definition of leadership, and that is true whether in the realm of the secular or of the sacred. Lord Montgomery said that his war experience led him to believe that the staff must be the servant of the troops, and that a good staff officer must serve his commander and troops, but must himself be anonymous.

In his *Training of the Twelve,* Dr. A. B. Bruce wrote: "In other kingdoms they rule, whose privilege it is to be ministered unto. In the Divine commonwealth, they rule who account it a privilege to minister." Dr. John A. MacKay of Princeton maintained that the servant image is the essential image of the Christian religion. The Son of God became the servant of God in order to fulfill the mission of God. That same image provides a pattern and norm whereby individual Christians, missionary societies, and Christian churches may learn how to fulfill their God-given mission.

The true leader regards the welfare of others rather than his own comfort and prestige as of primary concern. He manifests sympathy and concern for those under him in their problems, difficulties, and cares, but it is a sympathy that fortifies and stimulates, not that softens and weakens. He will always direct their confidence to the Lord. He sees in each emergency a new opportunity for helpfulness. It is noteworthy that when God chose a leader to follow the great Moses, He chose Joshua, the man who had proved himself a faithful servant (Exod. 33:11).

In an address giving some of the secrets of Hudson Taylor's remarkably successful leadership, his successor, D. E. Hoste, said:

> Another secret of his influence among us lay in his great sympathy and thoughtful consideration for the welfare and comfort of those about him. The high standard of self-sacrifice and toil which he ever kept before himself, never made him lacking in tenderness and sympathy toward those who were not able to go as far as he did in these respects. He manifested great tenderness and patience toward the failures and shortcomings of his brethren, and was thus able in many cases to help them reach a higher plane of devotion.[1]

To discipline is another responsibility of the leader, a responsibility that is onerous and often unwelcome. In any church or religious society there is the necessity to maintain godly and loving discipline if divine standards are to be maintained, especially in matters of soundness in the faith, morals, and Christian conduct.

Paul stipulates the spirit required in those who exercise discipline. "Brethren, even if a man is caught in any trespass, you who are *spiritual,* restore such a one in a spirit of gentleness; each one looking to yourself, lest you too be tempted" (Gal. 6:1, italics added). The fundamental requirement in all disciplinary action is *love*. "Admonish him as a brother" (2 Thess. 3:15). "I urge you to reaffirm your love for him" (2 Cor. 2:8). The person who has faced and honestly dealt with his own failures and shortcomings is best qualified to deal with the failures of others in a sympathetic and yet firm manner. The spirit of meekness will achieve far more than a critical and censorious spirit.

In approaching a matter that appears to require disciplinary action, five points should be borne in mind: (1) Such action should be taken only after the most thorough and impartial inquiry, (2) it should be undertaken only when it would be for the overall good of the work and the individual, (3) it should always be in a spirit of genuine love and conducted in the most considerate manner, (4) it should always be with the spiritual help and restoration of the offender in view, and (5) it should be done only with much prayer.

To guide is a third responsibility. The spiritual leader must know where he is going and, like the Eastern shepherd, go ahead of his flock. That was the method of the Chief Shepherd. "When he puts forth all his own, he goes before them, and the sheep follow him" (John 10:4). "The ideal leader," said A. W. Tozer, "is one who hears the voice of God, and beckons on as the voice calls him and them." Paul gave this challenge to the Corinthian Christians: "Be imitators of me, just as I also am of Christ" (1 Cor. 11:1). He knew who he was following and where he was going, and was therefore able to challenge them to follow him.

But it is not always a simple task to guide people who, though godly, have strong opinions of their own. The leader must not ruthlessly assert his will. D. E. Hoste emphasized that fact:

> In a mission like ours, those guiding its affairs must be prepared to put up with waywardness and opposition, and be able to desist from courses of action which, though they may be intrinsically sound and beneficial, are not approved by some of those affected. Hudson Taylor again and again was obliged either to greatly modify, or lay aside projects which were sound and helpful, but met with determined opposition, and so tended to create greater evils than those which might have been removed or miti-

gated by the changes in question. Later on, in answer to patient continuance in prayer, many of such projects were given effect to.[2]

To initiate is an important function of the office of a leader. Some have more gift for conserving gains than for initiating new ventures; more gift for achieving order than for generating ardor. The true leader must have venturesomeness as well as vision. He must be an initiator rather than a mere conserver. Most of us prefer to play safe, but Paul did not play safe. He constantly took carefully and prayerfully calculated risks.

The leader must either initiate plans for progress or recognize the plans of others. He must remain in front and give guidance and a sense of direction to those behind. He does not wait for things to happen, but makes them happen. He is a self-starter, and is always on the lookout for improved methods. He will be willing to test new ideas.

Robert Louis Stevenson indicted the attitude of safety, security, and prudence as "that dismal fungus."[3] Hudson Taylor did not play safe. The tremendous steps of faith that he took with monotonous regularity were denounced as wildcat schemes. But that did not deter him, and today history is on his side. The greatest achievements in the history of the church and of missions have been the outcome of some leader in touch with God taking courageous, carefully calculated risks.

A great deal more failure is the result of an excess of caution than of bold experimentation with new ideas. A friend who has filled with distinction an important post with global outreach in the Christian world recently remarked to the author that, in reviewing his life, he was surprised to discover that most of his failures were because he had not been sufficiently daring. "The frontiers of the kingdom of God were never advanced by men and women of caution," said Mrs. H. W. K. Mowll.[4]

A leader cannot afford to ignore the counsel of cautious men around him. They will often save him from unnecessary mistakes. But he must beware of allowing their excess of caution to curb his initiative, if he feels his vision is of God. Nor must he allow them to restrain him from taking daring steps of faith to which God is calling both him and them.

To undertake responsibility and do it willingly is a necessary mark of a leader. If he is not prepared for that, he disqualifies himself for office. One who evades the more onerous and difficult involvements incidental to his position limits his influence to that extent.

Joshua demonstrated his leadership quality in accepting without hesitation the awesome responsibility of following in the steps of the great leader Moses. Joshua had far greater reason to plead his inadequacy than did Moses, but he did not repeat the sin of his leader. Instead, he promptly accepted the responsibility and gave himself to the task.

When Elijah was translated, Elisha assumed without hesitation the responsibilities of the prophetic office vacated by his master. He accepted the authority conferred with the falling mantle and became a leader in his own right. In each case the determining factor was the assurance of a divine call. Granted that assurance, no one need hesitate to assume the responsibilities God allots.

It is always inspiring to be granted a glimpse into the inner life of great men of God and to know some of the elements that contributed to their spiritual effectiveness.

In the *Life of Robert E. Speer* are recorded the rules by which Archbishop Benson, a man carrying heavy responsibilities, conducted his life. They are both revealing and challenging. Although he belonged to a different age, many of his rules are of continuing relevance and merit our emulation.

• Not to be dilatory in commencing the day's main work.

• Not to murmur at the multitude of business or the shortness of time, but to buy up the time all around.

• Not to groan when letters are brought in; not even a murmur.

• Not to magnify undertaken duties by seeming to suffer under them, but to treat all as liberties and gladness.

• Not to call attention to crowded work or trivial experiences.

• Before censuring anyone, obtain from God a real love for him. Be sure that you know and that you allow all allowances that can be made. Otherwise, how ineffective, how unintelligible or perhaps provocative your best-meant censure may be.

• Oh, how well it doth make for peace to be silent about others, not to believe everything without discernment, and not to go on easily telling things.

• Not to seek praise, gratitude, respect, or regard from superiors or equals of age or past service.

• Not to feel uneasiness when your advice or opinion is not asked, or is set aside.

• Never to let yourself be placed in favorable contrast with another.

• Not to hunger for conversation to turn on yourself.

• To seek no favor, no compassion; to deserve, not ask for, tenderness.

• To bear blame rather than share or transmit it.

• When credit for your own design or execution is given to another, not to be disturbed, but to give thanks.

NOTES

1. Phyllis Thompson, *D. E. Hoste* (London: China Inland Mission, n.d.), p. 217.
2. Ibid., p. 158.
3. Robert Lewis Stevenson, in *The Reaper*, May 1961, p. 89.
4. Marcus Loane, *Archbishop Mowll* (London: Hodder & Stoughton, 1960), p. 249.

17

SEARCHING TESTS OF LEADERSHIP

God tested Abraham.

GENESIS 22:1

Then Jesus was led up by the Spirit into the wilderness to be tempted by the devil.

MATTHEW 4:1

There are tests to leadership as well as tests of leadership. "And . . . God did . . . [test] Abraham" is history expressing an eternal principle. To everyone entrusted with spiritual authority, searching tests are bound to come.

COMPROMISE

Compromise is the partial waiving of principle for the sake of reaching agreement. It is always a backward step when we consent to lower our standards, and all too often that is involved in arriving at a compromise. It nearly always involves a scaling down of standards.

The epic contest of Moses with Pharaoh affords a classic example of the progressive temptation to compromise. When Pharaoh discerned Moses' inflexible purpose to take Israel out of Egypt to worship the Lord, he used all his wiles to frustrate him. "Worship God if you will," was the first suggestion, "but there is no need to leave Egypt to do it. Worship God where you are." The modern counterpart would be: "Don't neglect religion. But there is no need to be narrow and make a complete break with the world."

When that approach failed, Pharaoh's suggestion was: "If you must go out of Egypt to worship, there is no need to go very far away. Just go outside the borders." "Religion is good and necessary, but you are not called on to be fanatical about it. Stay as near to the world as you can."

His next proposal played upon natural affection. "Let the men go and worship, but there is no need for the women and children to accompany them." "Break with the world yourself, if you must, but don't be so extreme as to interfere with the worldly advancement of your family by making them conform to your Victorian standards."

His final attempt was an appeal to their covetousness and love of material things: "Go if you must, but let your flocks and herds remain in Egypt while you go to worship." "Don't allow your legitimate religious convictions to conflict with your business interests and activities."

With clear spiritual insight Moses saw through

each specious suggestion, and his reply was clear-cut and decisive: "There shall not an hoof be left behind" (Exod. 8:25, 28; 10:11, 24, 26). So Moses passed with honors the first great test of his quality as a leader.

AMBITION

Like all great leaders, Moses was sifted by the test of ambition. When, during his absence on Mount Sinai alone with God, Israel turned to idolatry, the holy anger of the Lord was kindled. "I will smite them with pestilence and dispossess them, and I will make you into a nation greater and mightier than they" (Num. 14:12). Already Israel's chronic complaining and unbelief must have proved a great trial to Moses, and he might have been excused if he had seen in that divine proposal a lifting of his burdens and a wonderful opportunity for self-advancement.

Because it was God who initiated the suggestion, the test was the more searching. Never were Moses' selflessness and nobility of character more clearly seen than in his reaction to God's message. His concern was solely for God's glory and the people's welfare. Not for a moment did the thought of self-aggrandizement take root in his lofty mind. He held on to God audaciously and tenaciously; and through his intercession, judgment on the apostate nation was averted.

THE IMPOSSIBLE SITUATION

"How does he face impossible situations?" was one

of John R. Mott's tests for men of leadership caliber. It was his practice to encourage leaders to deal with impossible tasks rather than with easy ones, because that would draw out their powers, teach them their dependence on others, and drive them to God. "I long since ceased to occupy myself with minor things that can be done by others," he said. A true leader is at his best in baffling circumstances.

It would not be exaggeration to affirm that never in human history have leaders been confronted with such a concentration of unresolved crises and impossible situations as in our day. Consequently, if they are to survive, they must be able to thrive on difficulties and regard them as routine.

Moses faced the test of the impossible when Israel reached the Red Sea. On one side lay the impassable range of Baal Zephon, on the other side an impassable waste of sand. Before them lay the impassable Red Sea, behind them the invincible army of Pharaoh. He found himself shut up with a dismayed and complaining horde in a perfect cul-de-sac. In that unexpected and shattering experience the morale of the nation dropped below zero. "Is it because there were no graves in Egypt that you have taken us away to die in the wilderness?" they complained. But Moses, the man of faith, stayed himself on God. His order of the day sounded like sheer fantasy to the demoralized Israelites, but in point of fact it was a demonstration of superb leadership.

"Do not fear" he cried, when there was every reason to fear.

"Stand by!" when Pharaoh was rapidly overtaking them, and to stand still meant death.

"See the salvation of the LORD," which seemed a very long distance away (Exod. 14:11-13).

In that sublime declaration of faith, Moses passed the test of the impossible situation with first-class honors, and he was gloriously vindicated by God. His sanguine prediction came true: "The Egyptians whom you have seen today, you will never see them again forever." They saw the salvation of God and the total destruction of their enemies. The bracing lesson is that God delights to shut people up to Himself and then, in response to their trust, display His power and grace in doing the impossible.

In the evangelization of inland China, Hudson Taylor often found himself face to face with such situations. As a result of his experience he used to say that there were three phases in most great tasks undertaken for God—impossible, difficult, *done.*

Have you come to the Red Sea place in your
    life,
  Where in spite of all you can do,
There is no way out, there is no way back,
  There is no other way but through?
Then wait on the Lord with a trust serene
  Till the night of your fear is gone;
He will send the wind, He will heap the floods,
  When He says to your soul, "Go on."

And his hand will lead you through—clear
    through—

Ere the watery walls roll down,
No foe can reach you, no wave can touch,
No mightiest sea can drown;
The tossing billows may rear their crests,
Their foam at your feet may break,
But over their bed you shall walk dryshod
In the path that your Lord will make.

In the morning watch, 'neath the lifted cloud,
You shall see but the Lord alone,
When He leads you on from the place of the sea
To a land that you have not known;
And your fears shall pass as your foes have
passed,
You shall no more be afraid;
You shall sing His praise in a better place,
A place that His hand has made.

ANNIE JOHNSON FLINT*

FAILURE

If we could see into the inmost hearts of many men whom we think are riding on the crest of the wave, we should experience some great surprises. Alexander Maclaren, the peerless expositor, after delivering a wonderful address to a large gathering, went away overwhelmed with a sense of failure. "I must not speak on such an occasion again," he exclaimed, while the congregation went away blessed and inspired. Allowance must always be made for the reaction that comes from the rebound of the overstrung

*Used by permission of Evangelical Publishers, Toronto, Canada.

bow. Nor can we ignore the subtle attacks of our
unsleeping adversary.

The manner in which a leader meets his own failure will have a significant effect on his future ministry. One would have been justified in concluding
that Peter's failure in the judgment hall had forever
slammed the door on leadership in Christ's kingdom.
Instead, the depth of his repentance and the reality
of his love for Christ reopened the door of opportunity
to a yet wider sphere of service. "Where sin abounded,
grace did much more abound."

A study of Bible characters reveals that most of
those who made history were men who failed at some
point, and some of them drastically, but who refused
to continue lying in the dust. Their very failure and
repentance secured for them a more ample conception
of the grace of God. They learned to know Him as
the God of the second chance to His children who
had failed Him—and the third chance, too.

The historian Froude wrote, "The worth of a man
must be measured by his life, not by his failure under
a singular and peculiar trial. Peter the apostle, though
forewarned, thrice denied his Master on the first alarm
of danger; yet that Master, who knew his nature in its
strength and in its infirmity, chose him."

The successful leader is a man who has learned that
no failure need be final, and acts on that belief,
whether the failure is his own or that of another. He
must learn to be realistic and prepared to realize that
he cannot be right all the time. There is no such thing
as a perfect or infallible leader.

JEALOUSY

It is to be expected that at times leadership will be challenged by ambitious or jealous rivals. As his influence grew in its sweep, even the mighty Moses met with that experience. Disaffection is a common weapon of the adversary.

The first challenge to Moses' leadership came, tragically enough, from his loved sister and brother. They did not remember that but for his self-abnegating response to the divine call they would still have been smarting under the taskmaster's lash.

Miriam was by that time an elderly woman, whose experience of God should have taught her the evil and ugliness of jealousy. Apparently she had instigated a whispering campaign against Moses, using his marriage to an Ethiopian woman as an excuse to challenge his authority. Race hatred is no modern phenomenon. She resented being supplanted by a foreigner and drew the weak Aaron into the rebellion.

It is clear that Miriam and Aaron were not content to take second place to Moses, and at the instigation of Satan they attempted to oust him from his influential position. Their jealousy was piously cloaked in a simulated zeal for God. "Hath the Lord spoken only by Moses? Hath He not also spoken by us?" They refused to concede Moses' sole right to speak for God to the people.

Moses' reaction was exemplary. Though deeply wounded, he said nothing in vindication of himself, for his main concern was for the glory of God, not his own prestige. It was in that very connection that testimony was borne to his unique meekness. "The man Moses was very humble, more than any man who was on the face of the earth" (Num. 12:3). But although he maintained a dignified silence, God would not allow such a challenge to the authority of His servant to pass.

Because it was a public offense, it must be publicly judged and punished. "Behold, Miriam was leprous, as white as snow," the record runs. The drastic punishment from God indicated His estimate of the gravity of the sin of touching the Lord's anointed, frail and fallible man though he be. Once again Moses' greatness shines out. His only response was to intercede for his sister—intercession to which God graciously responded.

The lesson for the leader is plain. The man who is in the place of God's appointment need not attempt to vindicate himself when challenged by jealous rivals. That he is safe in the hands of his heavenly Protector, the Lord's rebuke to Miriam gives abundant confirmation. "Why then were you not afraid to speak against My servant Moses?" (12:8).

The second challenge came from Korah and his associates, who entertained an unreasoning jealousy of Moses and Aaron. Why should they alone enjoy the privileges of high office? Were there not others equally deserving and qualified, themselves included? Were Moses and Aaron the only ones fitted to mediate the message of God? "You have gone far enough," they charged, "for all the congregation are holy, every one of them, and the LORD is in their midst; so why do you exalt yourselves above the assembly of the LORD?" (Num. 16:3).

Although Moses once again refused to vindicate himself, God intervened and just judgment was meted out to the jealous dissidents. Fear fell on the people, and the prestige of Moses stood higher than ever.

God is jealous for the leaders whom He has called and appointed. He honors them, protects, and vindicates them, and relieves them of any necessity to stand up for their rights.

18

THE ART OF DELEGATION

*And Moses chose able men out of all Israel, and
made them heads over the people . . . and they
judged the people at all times; the difficult dis-
pute they would bring to Moses.*

EXODUS 18:25-26

One definition of leadership is the ability to recognize the special abilities and limitations of others,
combined with the capacity to fit each one into the
job where he will do his best. He who is successful
in getting things done through others is exercising the
highest type of leadership. That shrewd judge of
men Dwight L. Moody once said that he would
rather put a thousand men to work than do the work
of a thousand men. The ability to choose men to
whom he can safely delegate authority, and then actually to delegate it, is that of the true leader. General Director of the China Inland Mission, D. E.
Hoste said, "The capacity to appreciate the gifts of

widely varying kinds of workers, and then to help them along the lines of their own personalities and workings, is the main quality for oversight in a mission such as ours."[1]

That capacity will save the leader the frustrating experience of trying to fit square pegs into round holes.

Delegation of responsibility together with commensurate authority to enable that responsibility to be discharged is not always relished by one who enjoys exercising the authority himself. He is glad to devolve the responsibility, but reluctant to let the reins of power slip from his own hands. That is unfair to his subordinate and is unlikely to prove satisfactory or effective. Such an attitude would tend to be interpreted as indicating a lack of confidence, and that does not induce the best cooperation, nor will it draw out the highest powers of the one being trained for leadership. It is very possible that he may not do the task as well as his superior, but experience proves that that is by no means necessarily the case. Given the chance, the younger man may do it better because he is better able to feel the pulse of contemporary life. But in any case, how is he to gain experience unless both responsibility and authority are delegated to him?

"The degree to which a leader is able to delegate work is a measure of his success." It has been rightly contended that a one-person activity can never grow bigger than the greatest load that one person can carry. Some leaders feel threatened by brilliant subordinates and therefore are reluctant to delegate authority.

The man in a place of leadership who fails to delegate is constantly enmeshed in a morass of secondary detail that not only overburdens him but deflects him from his primary responsibilities. He also fails to release the leadership potential of those under him. To insist on doing things oneself because it will be done better is not only a short-sighted policy but may be evidence of an unwarranted conceit. The leader who is meticulous in observing priorities adds immeasurably to his own effectiveness.

Once delegation has been effected, he should manifest the utmost confidence in his colleagues. It was said of Dr. A. B. Simpson, founder of the Christian and Missionary Alliance, that he trusted those in charge of the different institutions and then left them free to exercise their own gifts.[2]

If they did not succeed, he believed it was a reflection on his own leadership, for it was he who selected them for that position. Subordinates should be utterly sure of their leader's support in any action they feel called upon to take, no matter what the result, so long as they have acted within their terms of reference. That presupposes that areas of responsibility have been clearly defined and committed to writing so that no misunderstanding can occur. Many unhappy situations have arisen through failure to do so.

Writing of his association with Dr. John R. Mott, Paul Super said:

> One of my greatest resources these ten years in Poland is the sense of his backing. My greatest pride is his belief in me. Surely one of my greatest motives is to be worthy of his support and to measure up to his expectations of me.[3]

The outstanding biblical illustration of the important principle of delegation of responsibility and authority is that of Jethro's advice to his son-in-law Moses, as recorded in Exodus 18:1-27.

Israel had emerged from Egypt, an unorganized horde of slaves. By that time a new national spirit was developing, and they were becoming an organized nation. The intolerable administrative burdens that that development imposed on Moses sparked Jethro's sound advice. From morn till night he saw Moses hearing and adjudicating on the endless problems that arose from the new conditions. Moses was saddled with both legislative and judicial functions, and his decisions were accepted by the people as the oracles of God.

Jethro saw that Moses could not endure the strain indefinitely and advanced two strong reasons in favor of delegation of some of his responsibilities. First, "You will surely wear out . . . the task is too heavy for you, you cannot do it alone" (v. 18). There are limits to the expenditure of physical and nervous force beyond which it is not safe to go. Second, the present method was too slow, and the people were getting dissatisfied because they were not receiving the attention they desired. Sharing responsibility would speed up legal decisions, and the people would go away satisfied (v. 23).

Jethro then proposed a twofold course of action. Moses should continue to act as God's representative, teaching spiritual principles and exercising his legislative functions. It would be for him to bring the hard cases to God (vv. 16, 19-20). He should delegate the judicial functions that he had hitherto exercised to competent legal officers who could thus lighten his intolerable burden. It was wise advice, for had Moses succumbed to the strain of his office, he would have left behind him no one experienced and trained in the exercise of authority and the bearing of responsibility. Failure to make such provision has spelled ruin to many a promising work of God.

Several benefits accrued to Moses through following Jethro's advice. He was able to concentrate on the higher aspects and responsibilities of his office. The latent and unsuspected talents of many of his subordinates were discovered. Those gifted men, who might have become his critics had he continued to keep things in his own hands, were developed by the burden of their office and became his staunch allies. Incipient disaffection was stifled by the speeding up of legal processes. He also made provision for the effective leadership of the nation after his death.

Jethro encouraged his son-in-law by stating a spiritual principle of timeless relevance. "If you do this thing, and God so commands you, then you will be able to endure" (Exod. 18:23). He submitted his advice to the ultimate direction of God. The principle is that God assumes full responsibility for enabling His man to fulfill every task to which He has appointed him. There are some self-imposed tasks that others can do better than we can, and we should relinquish them. But even should they do them worse, we should still relinquish them—a severe test for the perfectionist! Moses could doubtless have done the task better than the seventy men whom he selected, but had he persisted in doing so, he would soon have been only a memory.

Jethro's suggested standards of selection of helpers for Moses evidenced true spiritual discernment. They must be men of *ability*, for theirs would be an exacting task; men of *piety,* who feared God and respected their fellowmen; men of *honor,* who hated covetousness and would not be susceptible to bribery.

Among other lessons for leaders in the incident are these: It is a mistake to assume more duties than we can adequately and satisfactorily discharge. There is no virtue in doing more than our fair share of the work. It is good to be able to recognize and accept our own limitations. Our Jethros can often discern, more clearly than we, the cost at which our leadership is being exercised, and we would be wise to heed their admonitions. If we break natural law, even in the service of God, we are not exempted from its penalties. It is easy to assume responsibilities under pressure from men rather than by direction from God. For such extracurricular activities God accepts no responsibility.

One of the acid tests of missionary leadership is

willingness to delegate responsibility to emerging national leaders the moment they evidence sufficient spiritual maturity, and then to stand by, ready to help, while they gain experience in the same way as the missionary did, by trial and error. Such devolving of responsibility fulfills the important function of discovering, training, and using the latent talent of national colleagues. In the earlier stages, a wise watchfulness will be necessary, but a resort to interference should be made only if the need becomes acute. The sense of being watched destroys confidence.

When Dr. W. E. Sangster was appointed general secretary of the Home Mission Department of the Methodist Church of Britain, he arranged the division of labor between all the members of his department and assigned to each responsibilities over which he gave up all supervision. Trusting his colleagues absolutely, he delegated his powers and never regretted it. It was said of him: "Perhaps his greatest grasp of leadership was knowing the importance of delegation and of choosing assistants with care. He was always a master of that art."[4]

Writing of the leader of a large missionary society, a member of his staff commented: "He had a great gift of leadership in that he never interfered with those who worked under him. Everyone was left to do his own work." Another member wrote, "He knew what people could do, and saw that they did it, leaving them to make the best of their opportunities, and investigating only if things went wrong."[5]

NOTES

1. Phyllis Thompson, *D. E. Hoste* (London: China Inland Mission, n.d.), p. 156.
2. A. E. Thompson, *The Life of A. B. Simpson* (Harrisburg: Christian Publications, 1920), p. 208.
3. B. Matthews, *John R. Mott* (London: Hodder & Stoughton, 1909), p. 364.
4. Paul E. Sangster, *Doctor Sangster* (London: Epworth, 1962), pp. 88, 221.
5. Phyllis Thompson, *Climbing on Track* (London: China Inland Mission, 1954), p. 99.

19

THE REPLACEMENT OF LEADERS

Moses my servant is dead; now therefore arise, cross this Jordan, you and all this people. . . . Just as I have been with Moses, I will be with you.

Joshua 1:2, 5

When a movement develops around a dominant personality, the real test of the quality of his leadership is the manner in which that work survives the crisis of his removal. That fact was tacitly recognized by Gamaliel when he counseled his fellow Pharisees: "Stay away from these men, and let them alone, for if this plan of action should be of men, it will be overthrown; but if it is of God, you will not be able to overthrow them" (Acts 5:38-39). A work originated by God and conducted on spiritual principles will surmount the shock of a change of leadership and indeed will probably thrive better as a result.

It is possible to entertain an unholy solicitude for God and His work. The death of one of His workmen does not take Him by surprise and cause Him to take emergency action. Even though we may be taken unawares and shattered by the removal, we need not tremble for the Ark of God. We must bear in mind that there are factors in Christian leadership that are absent from that of the world. In the ultimate it is God and not man who prepares and selects those who are to assume positions of leadership in His kingdom (Mark 10:40). No work that He has initiated will be left unprovided for until His purpose through it has been achieved.

It has been asserted that every great movement is thrown into crisis on the death of its founder. While that may be true, the crisis is by no means always fatal. When the first secretary of the American Board of Missions died, Lyman Beecher said he inclined to despair of the future of the work of their foreign missions. But another took up the work so admirably that his death brought the same temptation. At last, when the third secretary proved himself the equal of his predecessors, Dr. Beecher began to think that God's resources were quite equal to taking care of the board and its affairs. When he himself was laid aside, some mourned it as an irreplaceable loss to temperance, to orthodoxy, and to foreign missions. But all those causes found new leaders in God's time and way.[1] The fact is that no man, however gifted and devoted, is indispensable to the work of the kingdom.

God is always at work, unperceived by men, preparing those of His choice for leadership. When the crisis arises, He dexterously fits His appointee into the place He has ordained for him. It is often true that the replacement for a certain position is not immediately obvious to those concerned, but time will reveal him.

Not the promised land, but men like Moses and David and Isaiah were God's greatest gifts to Israel, for His greatest gifts are always men. His greatest endowment to His church was the gift of twelve men whom He had trained for leadership.

It is not difficult to picture the dismay and even despair that gripped the nation when the time drew near for the firm, capable hand of Moses to be withdrawn from the helm. For four decades the whole national life had revolved around him. It was to him they had looked for the solution of their problems and the settlement of their disputes. It was he who had interpreted the will of God to them. They could be forgiven for feeling that he was irreplaceable. True, there were the seventy elders who served under him, but there was not another Moses on the horizon. The fact that his death occurred at the very moment they were about to enter Canaan imparted added acuteness to the crisis. They found it hard to believe that God had in reserve the very man to meet the emergency. But God had long been preparing Joshua. It only took the crisis to bring him to the fore.

That situation constantly recurs in history, and each generation has to learn the same lesson for itself. The loss of an outstanding leader always awakens the same doubts and fears. "What will happen to Methodism when John Wesley dies?" "What will happen to the Salvation Army when William Booth dies?" "What will happen when our pastor moves?"

The paths of glory ever lead but to the grave, but a new glory will be revealed. The greatest leader must inevitably be removed by death or some other cause, and the sense of loss will vary with the caliber of his leadership. But in retrospect it will usually be seen that the seeming tragedy has actually turned out to be in the best interests of the work.

Only after his removal are the character and achievements of a leader fully revealed. It was not until after Moses' death that Israel saw his greatness in its true perspective. "The emphasis of death makes perfect the lessons of the life."

On the other hand, the removal of a leader cuts him down to size in relation to the work of God. However great his achievements, he is not irreplaceable. The time comes when his special contribution is not the need of the hour. The most gifted leader has limitations that become apparent only after the complementary gifts of his successor cause the work to develop along lines for which the former leader was unfitted. It frequently emerges that a smaller man with different gifts can develop a work more effectively than his predecessor who initiated it. Moses may well have been unable to achieve the conquest and division of Canaan as ably and acceptably as Joshua.

The removal of a strong and dominating leader makes for the emergence and development of new leadership. It is often discovered that one who has been in a subordinate position develops totally unsuspected qualities when the weight of responsibility is thrown upon him. Latent powers and capacities that others have never suspected are awakened. Joshua would never have been the outstanding leader he subsequently proved to be had he remained "Moses' minister."

A shift of leadership also provides opportunity for the display of the versatility of God in adapting the means to the end in view. His resources in any work He initiates are inexhaustible. If a man possessing great gifts will not place them at the disposal of God, He is not defeated. He will take a man of lesser gifts that are fully available to Him and will supplement them with His own mighty power. That thought is implicit in Paul's intriguing statement to the brilliant Corinthians: "For consider your calling, brethren, that there were not many wise according to the flesh, not many mighty, not many noble; but God has chosen the foolish things of the world to shame the wise, and God has chosen the weak things of the world to shame the things which are strong, and the base things of the world, and the despised, God has chosen, the things that are not, that He might nullify the things that are, that no man should boast before God" (1 Cor. 1:26-29).

It is not that God does not desire to use the powers of the nobly gifted, but that few of them are as willing as was Paul to place those gifts without reservation at God's disposal. When such men renounce reliance on their own power and wisdom and depend on God's, there is no limit to the way in which He will use them for His glory.

Toward the end of the life of the greatly gifted Dr. A. B. Simpson, founder of the Christian and Missionary Alliance, a prominent New York minister suggested at one of Dr. Simpson's great conventions that, as there was no one similarly qualified to continue leadership of the organization, a large endowment fund should be raised to ensure the perpetuation of the work. Dr. Simpson said nothing and did nothing. He rightly believed that if the work was of God, nothing could overthrow it, and if it were not of God, no good purpose would be served by perpetuating it.[2]

How he rejoiced during the last months of his life, when he had no part in the leadership of the Alliance, to receive reports of largely increased missionary offerings and marvelous progress on the foreign fields. The year after his death proved to be the most prosperous in the history of the society. No greater tribute could be paid to the quality of his leadership.

There is one Leader who holds office in perpetuity, for whom no replacement is needed. It is a striking fact that His disciples made no move to appoint one of their number to take His place after His ascension, tacit evidence that they were gloriously conscious that He was still their living Leader. The church at times has lost the vivid sense of His presence, but there has never been the panic cry of a leaderless army. He has always demonstrated that the distresses and perils of His church lie deeply on His heart.

"We tell our Lord plainly," said Martin Luther, "that if He will have His Church then He must look to and maintain and defend it, for we can neither uphold nor protect it; and if we could, then we should become the proudest asses under heaven."

Since we have a Leader who conducts His work in the power of an endless life, the same yesterday, and today, and forever, changes in human leadership need not shake or dismay us.

NOTES

1. *Sunday School Times*, 8 November 1913, p. 682.
2. A. E. Thompson, *The Life of A. B. Simpson* (Harrisburg: Christian Publications, 1920), p. 208.

20

THE REPRODUCTION OF LEADERS

The things you have heard from me in the presence of many witnesses, these entrust to faithful men, who will be able to teach others too.

2 TIMOTHY 2:2

In those words Paul presses home the responsibility of the spiritual leader to reproduce and multiply himself. If he is to discharge his trust fully he will devote time to training younger men to succeed and perhaps even supersede him. The spiritual stature of Barnabas is seen in his entire freedom from jealously when his brilliant protégé, Paul, outstripped him and became the dominant member of the team. It follows that the leader must give his subordinates adequate scope for the exercise and development of their powers.

It was John R. Mott's contention that leaders must seek to multiply their lives by developing younger

men, by giving them full play and adequate outlet for
their powers. In order to achieve that, heavy burdens
of responsibility should be laid on them, including increasing opportunities of initiative and power of final
decision. They should be given recognition and generous credit for their achievements. The principal
thing is to trust them. Blunders are the inevitable
price of training leaders.

At a recent conference of missionaries, a national
leader was invited to express frankly, from an Asian
standpoint, what he considered to be the role of the
missionary in the world of today. Among other things
he said: "The missionary of today in the Orient should
cease to be so much a performer, and become more a
trainer." Although that is, of course, not true in every
missionary situation, it does highlight one of the great
needs in current missionary strategy.

The task of training prospective leaders is a delicate one, requiring considerable finesse. The wise
leader will not advertise the end he has in view. Out
of his wide experience, Bishop Stephen Neill pin-
pointed some of the dangers of a wrong approach to
that vital aspect of Christian work: "If we set out to
produce a race of leaders, what we shall succeed in
doing is probably to produce a race of restless, ambitious and discontented intellectuals. To tell a man he
is called to be a leader is the best way of ensuring his
spiritual ruin, since in the Christian world ambition
is more deadly than any other sin, and, if yielded to,
makes a man unprofitable in the ministry. The most
important thing today is the spiritual, rather than the

intellectual, quality of those indigenous Christians who are called to bear responsibility in the younger churches."

Bishop Leslie Newbigin even goes so far as to question how far the conception of leadership is one that we really ought to encourage. It is so difficult to use it without being misled by its non-Christian counterpart. The need is not so much for leaders as for saints and servants, and unless that fact is held steadily in the foreground, the whole idea of leadership training becomes dangerous. The pattern of training in Christian leadership must still be that given by our Lord in His training of the twelve.[1]

Perhaps the most strategic and fruitful work of the missionary in the contemporary world is to aid the leaders of tomorrow in developing their spiritual potential. It is a task that requires careful thought, wise planning, endless patience, and genuine Christian love. It should not be left haphazard. Our Lord devoted the greater part of His three years of ministry to molding the characters and disciplining the spirits of His disciples. Time was no object in that essential work. Paul trod in the steps of his Lord in training such promising young men as Timothy and Titus.

His method of preparing Timothy for the responsibility of ministering to the well-taught Ephesian church is deeply instructive. Timothy would have been about twenty years of age when his tutelage began. He had been brought up in a feminine atmosphere, and a tendency to effeminacy was probably accentuated by his own indifferent health. His innate timidity, too, required correction. The record indicates that he needed more iron in his makeup. There was a tendency to be desultory about his work and to be overtolerant and partial with important people. He could be petulant and irritable with opponents. He was apt to rely on an old spiritual experience instead of rekindling its dying flame. But Paul had very high and exacting aspirations for him, and did not spare him experiences or shelter him from hardships that would toughen his fiber and impart virility. He did not hesitate to assign to him tasks beyond his powers. How else could a young man develop greater capacity than by tackling tasks that extended him to the utmost?[2]

Traveling with Paul would bring Timothy into contact with men of all kinds, men of stature, whose personalities and achievements would kindle in him a wholesome ambition. From his tutor he learned how to meet triumphantly the crises that seemed routine in Paul's life and ministry. He was accorded the privilege of sharing the preaching. He was entrusted with the responsibility of establishing the group of Christians at Thessalonica and confirming them in the faith. Nor did he fail to justify that expression of confidence. Paul's exacting standards, high expectations and heavy demands served to bring out the best in Timothy and probably saved him from mediocrity.

Dr. Paul S. Rees tells of a journey he took in Bolivia with the Reverend Samuel Escobar. "He was reading a paperback book," said Dr. Rees, "which, quite obviously, he found absorbingly interesting.

After some low mutterings of excitement, he roused my curiosity. The book was entitled *Dedication and Leadership Techniques*. Its author is an Englishman by the name of Douglas Hyde, for twenty years an active, agitating, organizing member of the communist party. In 1948 he experienced a conversion, renounced Marxism, and became an active, witnessing Roman Catholic Christian.

> Easily one of the most fascinating stories in the book—a story connected with his Communist years—involves a young man who came to Douglas Hyde and announced that he wanted to be made into a leader. "I thought," said Hyde, "I had never seen anyone look less like a leader in my life. He was short, grotesquely fat, with a great, flabby, wide, uninteresting face. . . . He had a cast in one eye," and spoke "with a most distressing stutter."
>
> What happened? Well, instead of turning him away as a hopeless prospect, Hyde gave him a chance—a chance to study, to learn, to test his dedication, to smooth out his stutter. In the end he became one of the leaders in one of the most Communist-infiltrated labour unions in Britain.[3]

The observant leader may discover latent leadership qualities in some quite unprepossessing people.

Altogether apart from the merits of his movement, Frank Buchman, founder of Moral Rearmament, displayed a flair for leadership. It was his claim that if he did not train others to do what he had been doing better than he did it, he would have failed. For many years he worked to make himself dispensable, and it was in doing so that he differed from many other leaders.[4]

On the mission fields no work is more important and rewarding than that, for on the spiritual caliber and training of the national Christians will depend the development of the church. Once the initial pioneer stage in any field has been passed, that phase of the work should have high priority. The multiplying of himself in the lives of the promising young people among whom he works should rank as one of the main goals of the missionary.

In the training of younger missionaries for leadership, room should be left for flexibility in the case of the exceptional or unusual missionary. God has His "irregulars," and many of them have made an outstanding contribution to the evangelization of the world. Who could have poured Charles T. Studd into any one mold? Such men and women cannot be measured by ordinary standards or made to conform to any fixed pattern.

One such missionary was Douglas Thornton, who made an indelible mark in his work among Muslims in the Near East. He was a man of rare gifts, and even as a raw recruit he did not hesitate to express views that to his seniors seemed radical and impracticable,

His biographer writes:

> It is hardly surprising to learn that he felt constrained to write to his society a memorandum setting forth his views on the past, present and future of the work in Egypt. It is not a precedent

that young missionaries after three and a half months on the field should be invited to follow, and on this occasion, too, heads were shaken. But Thornton was an exceptional man, and time has proved that his views and even his effusions were worthy of being studied. It was never safe to neglect them. Most juniors had best reserve their observations for a more mature season. But when the exceptional man arrives, two things have to be observed—the man has to learn to make his observations in the right way, so as to carry his seniors with him; the seniors have to learn how to learn from one who is possibly able, in spite of his want of local knowledge, to benefit them enormously by his fresh and spontaneous ideas. Each is a difficult lesson.[5]

It remains to be said that the training of leaders cannot be done by employing the techniques of mass production. It will require patient and careful instruction and prayerful and personal guidance of the individual over a considerable period. "Disciples are not manufactured wholesale. They are produced one by one, because someone has taken the pains to discipline, to instruct and enlighten, to nurture and train one that is younger."

When a man is really marked out by God for leadership, He will see to it that he receives the necessary disciplines to make him effective.

> When God wants to drill a man
> And thrill a man
> And skill a man,

When God wants to mold a man
  To play the noblest part;
When He yearns with all His heart
  To create so great and bold a man
That all the world shall be amazed,
  Watch His methods, watch His ways!
How He ruthlessly perfects
  Whom He royally elects!
How He hammers him and hurts him,
  And with mighty blows converts him
Into trial shapes of clay which
  Only God understands;
While his tortured heart is crying
  And he lifts beseeching hands!
How He bends but never breaks
  When his good He undertakes;
How He uses whom He chooses
  And with every purpose fuses him;
  By every act induces him
To try His splendour out—
  God knows what He's about!

AUTHOR UNKNOWN

NOTES

1. Bishop Leslie Newbigin, in *International Review of Missions*, April 1950.
2. H. C. Lees, *St. Paul's Friends* (London: Religious Tract Society, 1917), pp. 135-41.
3. Paul S. Rees, "The Community Clue," *Life of Faith*, 26 September 1976, p. 3.
4. P. Howard, *Frank Buchman* (London: Heineman, 1961), p. 111.
5. W. H. T. Gairdner, *Douglas M. Thornton* (London: Hodder & Stoughton, n.d.), p. 121.

21

THE PECULIAR PERILS OF LEADERSHIP

Lest possibly, after I have preached to others, I myself should be disqualified.

1 CORINTHIANS 9:27

Although there are occupational hazards in all callings, the perils of the spiritual leader are especially subtle. He is by no means immune to the temptations of the flesh, but the dangers most to be guarded against lie in the realm of the spirit. He must remember that "Sabbathless Satan," his relentless enemy, will take advantage of every inch of ground he concedes in any area of his life.

PRIDE

The very fact that a man has risen to a position of leadership with its attendant prominence tends to engender a secret self-congratulation and pride which, if not checked, will unfit him for further advancement in the service of the kingdom, for "everyone who is proud in heart is an abomination to the LORD" (Prov. 16:5). Strong and searching words, those! Nothing is more distasteful to God than self-conceit. That first and fundamental sin in essence aims at enthroning self at the expense of God. It was the sin that changed the anointed cherub, guardian of the throne of God, into the foul fiend of hell, and caused his expulsion from heaven.

Of the myriad forms that that sin assumes, none is more abhorrent than spiritual pride. To be proud of spiritual gifts that God has bestowed or of the position to which His love and grace have elevated us, is to forget that grace is a gift, and that all we have has been received.

Pride is a sin of whose presence its victim is least conscious. There are, however, three tests by means of which it can soon be discovered whether or not we have succumbed to its blandishments.

The test of precedence. How do we react when another is selected for the assignment we expected or for the office we coveted? When another is promoted and we are overlooked? When another outshines us in gifts and accomplishments?

The test of sincerity. In our moments of honest self-criticism we will say many things about ourselves and really mean them. But how do we feel when others, especially our rivals, say exactly the same things about us?

The test of criticism. Does criticism arouse hostility and resentment in our hearts and cause us to fly to immediate self-justification? Do we hasten to criticize the critic?

If we are honest, when we measure ourselves by the life of our Lord who humbled Himself even to death on a cross, we cannot but be overwhelmed with the tawdriness and shabbiness, and even the vileness, of our hearts. As we see our pride in its true colours, our cry will be:

> Boasting excluded, pride I abase;
> I'm only a sinner, saved by grace.
>
> JAMES M. GRAY

EGOTISM

Egotism is one of the repulsive manifestations of pride. It is the practice of thinking and speaking much of oneself, the habit of magnifying one's attainments or importance. It leads one to consider everything in its relation to himself rather than in relation to God and the welfare of His people. The leader who has for long been admired and deferred to by his followers is in great danger of succumbing to this peril.

When Robert Louis Stevenson arrived in Samoa, he was invited by the head of the Malua Institute for training native pastors to address the students. He willingly consented. His address was based on the Muslim story of the veiled prophet. That prophet, a burning and shining light among the teachers of his peo-

ple, wore a veil over his face because, he said, the
glory of his countenance was so great that no one
could bear the sight.

But at last the veil grew old and fell into decay.
Then the people discovered that he was only an ugly
old man trying to hide his own ugliness. Stevenson
went on to enforce the need of sincerity on the ground
that, however high the truths the preacher taught, and
however skillfully he might excuse blemishes of character, the time comes when the veil falls away, and
a man is seen by people as he really is. It is seen
whether beneath the veil is the ugly face of unmorti-
fied egotism or the transfigured glory of Christlike
character.

> It is a good test to the rise and fall of egotism
> to notice how you listen to the praises of other
> men of your own standing. Until you can listen
> to the praises of a rival without any desire to
> indulge in detraction or any attempt to belittle
> his work, you may be sure there is an unmorti-
> fied prairie of egotistic impulse in your nature
> yet to be brought under the grace of God.[1]

JEALOUSY

Jealousy is a near relative of pride. The jealous
person is apprehensive and suspicious of rivals. That
temptation came to Moses through the touching loyalty of his own colleagues. "Eldad and Medad are
prophesying in the camp." Said the outraged Joshua
to his master, "Moses, my lord, restrain them" (Num.
11:28). Those two from among the men whom

Moses had appointed to assist him had broken into prophecy, and his loyal followers were jealous on his behalf at the usurping of his prophetic prerogatives and challenge to his prestige. But envy and jealousy found no culture-bed in the generous nature of the man who used to speak with God face to face. Such matters could safely be left with the God who had called him.

"Are you jealous for my sake?" was his untroubled rejoinder. "Would that all the LORD's people were prophets." The leader who is jealous for God's glory need have no concern for his own prestige and prerogatives. They are safe in His hands.

POPULARITY

The cult of the personality is not confined to Communism. In Paul's day it reared its head in Corinth, and it is with us today. There will always be those unwise souls who accord an undue deference to their spiritual leaders and advisers, and who tend to exalt one above another.

That practice was prevalent in Corinth and caused Paul to write: "When one says, 'I am of Paul,' and another, 'I am of Apollos,' are you not mere men? What then is Apollos? And what is Paul? Servants through whom you believed, even as the Lord gave opportunity to each one. I planted, Apollos watered, but God was causing the growth. . . . We are God's fellow-workers" (1 Cor. 3:4-6, 9).

An exaggerated deference to leaders in the church is a mark of spiritual immaturity and carnality. And an acceptance of such fawning deference by the leader is an evidence of the very same weaknesses. Paul was shocked by it and vigorously repudiated it. It is not wrong to be greatly loved by those whom one has endeavored to serve, but there is always the danger that devotion may be deflected from the Master to the servant. Spiritual leaders are to be "esteemed very highly in love for their work's sake," but that esteem should not degenerate into adulation.

That leader is most successful who attaches the affection of his followers more to Christ than to himself. He can rightly draw encouragement from the fact that his service has been fruitful and appreciated, but he must sedulously refuse to be idolized.

What leader or preacher does not desire to be popular with his constituency? Certainly there is no virtue in unpopularity, but popularity can be purchased at too high a price. Jesus made that crystal-clear when He said, "Woe unto you when all men speak well of you." And He expressed the complementary truth when He said, "Blessed are ye when men revile you and persecute you, and utter all kinds of evil against you falsely for my sake."

Bishop Stephen Neill said, in an address to theological students, "Popularity is the most dangerous spiritual state imaginable, since it leads on so easily to the spiritual pride which drowns men in perdition. It is a symptom to be watched with anxiety since so often it has been purchased at the too heavy price of compromise with the world."[2]

The dangers of popularity and success were constantly before Spurgeon in his unique ministry.

> Success exposes a man to the pressure of people and thus tempts him to hold on to his gains by means of fleshly methods and practices, and to let himself be ruled wholly by the dictatorial demands of incessant expansion. Success can go to my head, and will unless I remember that it is God who accomplishes the work, that He can continue to do so without my help, and that He will be able to make out with other means whenever He cuts me down to size.[3]

Wherever he went, the popularity of George Whitefield was immense. However, he lived to grow tired of his popularity and often envied the man who could enter a restaurant and take his choice of food with no one to think of his presence. But he had not always felt that way. In the early days of his career he said that to him it was death to be despised and worse than death to think of being laughed at. "But I have seen enough of popularity to be sick of it," he declared.

To one who warned him to beware of the evils of popularity he replied, "I thank you heartily. May God reward you for watching over my soul; and as to what my enemies say against me, I know worse things of myself than they say about me."[4]

INFALLIBILITY

Spirituality does not equate infallibility. The fact that a person is indwelt by the Spirit and seeks to be led by the Spirit will doubtless mean that he is less liable to make mistakes than those who do not; but since he is still in the flesh, he is not infallible. Even the divinely called and Spirit-filled apostles made mistakes that required divine overruling.

The leader who knows God, and probably knows Him better than his colleagues, is in danger of falling unconsciously into this subtle peril. Because his judgment has usually proved more accurate than theirs, because he has prayed and thought and wrestled with the problem more earnestly than they, it is difficult for him to concede the possibility of mistake and to yield to the judgment of his brethren. He must be a man of conviction and be prepared to stand for what he believes, but that is different from assuming virtual infallibility. Willingness to concede the possibility of an error of judgment and to defer to the judgment of one's brethren enhances rather than diminishes influence. Infallibility results in loss of confidence. It is strange but true that such an attitude can coexist with a genuine humility in other areas of life.

INDISPENSABILITY

Many who have wielded great influence fall before the temptation to think that they are irreplaceable and that in the best interests of the work they should not relinquish office. They cling to authority long after it should have been passed on to younger men. In no sphere is that disastrous tendency more prevalent than in Christian work. Advance is held up for years by well-meaning but aging men who refuse to vacate office and insist on holding the reins in their failing hands. The author met a fine Christian of nearly ninety years of age who was still superintendent of the Sunday school of a city church. And it was not because there were no younger men available. Apparently no officials in the church were courageous enough to handle the situation realistically. Unfortunately there are well-intentioned people who encourage such men in the myth of their indispensability, and as we get older we become progressively less able to assess our own contribution objectively.

The missionary who has made himself indispensable to the church he has helped into being has done it a grave disservice. From earliest days it should have been his studied aim to remain in the background, to cultivate in its members a real dependence on the Lord, and to train spiritual men who, as soon as practicable, could assume complete responsibility for the work.

ELATION AND DEPRESSION

In every work for God there are inevitably times of discouragement and frustration as well as days of uplift and achievement. The leader is in peril of being unduly depressed by the one and unduly elated by the other. Nor is it always easy to discover the mean between the two.

The seventy disciples returned from their mission, highly elated with their success. Jesus quickly checked this natural but soulish reaction. "Do not rejoice in this, that the spirits are subject to you," He admon-

ished them, "but rejoice that your names are recorded
in heaven" (Luke 10:20). He directed their attention to the fate of the exalted being who let high privilege go to his head. "I was watching Satan fall from
heaven like lightning."

After the drama on Carmel, Elijah experienced
such acute depression that he wished to die. The
Lord corrected his morbid, self-pitying reactions in a
very prosaic manner. He did not approach his over-
wrought prophet with a spiritual probe or scalpel. Instead, He made him take two long sleeps and eat two
square meals. Only then did He begin to deal with
the deeper spiritual problem—a lesson of abiding
value. He was then able to show Elijah that no real
basis for his discouragement existed. There were still
seven thousand of his compatriots who had never
bowed the knee to Baal. By fleeing, he had deprived
the nation of the leadership of which it was in desperate need.

It is realistic to face the fact that not all our ideals
for God's work will be realized. Cherished idols prove
to have feet of clay. People on whom we lean will
prove broken reeds. Even leadership that has been
deeply sacrificial will sometimes be challenged. But
the spiritually mature leader will know how to discern
the true origin of depression and discouragement and
will deal with it accordingly.

> Most people who knew Dr. F. B. Meyer
> would have no hesitation in writing him down
> as a convinced optimist, ever seeing the bright
> side of things, ever hopeful, ever vigorous, ever

confident of the ultimate triumph of good over evil. And they would have been right. He was delightfully hopeful and inspiring. But he was far too keen and thoughtful a man, too great a student of humanity, and in himself he was unmeasurably human not to be overcome now and again by the pessimistic views of life. He occasionally went down into the very depths of human despair. He had seen too often and too clearly the seamy side of life not to be sad and pessimistic now and then.[5]

He was a man of like passions, but he never stayed long in the depths.

There can be depression of another kind, as C. H. Spurgeon testified in his lecture "The Minister's Fainting Fits":

Before any great achievement, some measure of depression is very usual. . . . Such was my experience when I first became a pastor in London. My success appalled me, and the thought of the career which seemed to open up so far from elating me, cast me into the lowest depth, out of which I muttered my *miserere* and found no room for a *gloria in excelsis*. Who was I that I should continue to lead so great a multitude? I would betake me to my village obscurity, or emigrate to America and find a solitary nest in the backwoods where I might be sufficient for the things that were demanded of me. It was just then the curtain was rising on my lifework, and I dreaded what it might reveal. I hope I was not faithless, but I was timorous and filled with

> a sense of my own unfitness. . . . This depression
> comes over me whenever the Lord is preparing
> a larger blessing for my ministry.[6]

There are seasons when everything goes well.
Goals are reached, planned endeavors are crowned
with success, the Spirit moves, souls are saved and
saints blessed. In those times the mature leader knows
on whose brow to place the crown of achievement.
When Robert Murray McCheyne experienced times
of blessing in his ministry, on returning home from
the service, he would kneel down and symbolically
place the crown of success on the brow of the Lord,
to whom he knew it rightly belonged. That practice
helped to save him from the peril of arrogating to
himself the glory that belonged to God alone.

Samuel Chadwick summed up the wise attitude to
that peril in these cryptic words: "If successful, don't
crow; if defeated don't croak."[7]

PROPHET OR LEADER?

Sometimes there is a conflict between two minis-
tries, for each of which a man is fitted. For example,
a preacher who possesses marked gifts of leadership
may reach a place in his church or organization that
compels him to choose whether his role is to be one
of popular leader or unpopular prophet.

Such a dilemma was pictured by Dr. A. C. Dixon,
who was pastor of the Moody Church in Chicago, and
later of Spurgeon's Tabernacle in London:

Every preacher ought to be primarily a prophet of God who preaches as God bids him, without regard to results. When he becomes conscious of the fact that he is a leader in his own church or denomination, he has reached a crisis in his ministry. He must now choose one of two courses, that of prophet of God or a leader of men. If he seeks to be a prophet and a leader, he is apt to make a failure of both. If he decides to be a prophet only insofar as he can do without losing his leadership, he becomes a diplomat and ceases to be a prophet at all. If he decides to maintain leadership at all costs, he may easily fall to the level of a politician who pulls the wires in order to gain or hold a position.[8]

Of course there is not such a clear-cut dichotomy between the two roles as Dr. Dixon suggests, and the one does not necessarily exclude the other. But a situation can very easily develop in which one has to choose between a spiritual ministry and a leadership that would prevent its highest exercise. Herein lies the peril.

Dr. Reuben A. Torrey, whom God used at the turn of the century to bring revival to half the world, was faced with such a choice. Dr. Dixon wrote of him:

The thousands who have heard Dr. Torrey know the man and his message. He loves the Bible, and believing it to be the infallible Word of God, preaches it with the fervor of red-hot conviction. He never compromises. *He has chosen to be a prophet of God rather than a*

mere leader of men, and that is the secret of his
power with God and men.[9]

DISQUALIFICATION

Even his glowing record of sacrifice and boundless
success in the service of Christ could not quiet in
Paul's heart a wholesome fear that after having
preached to others, he might himself be disqualified
(1 Cor. 9:27). To him it was an ever-present challenge and warning, as it should be to all entrusted with
spiritual responsibilities. High attainment and vast
experience did not engender in Paul a smug complacency, nor did he consider himself immune to such
a dire anticlimax to his life of sacrificial service.

The word translated "castaway" or "disapproved"
is used of metals, and has reference to that which,
having been tested, fails to survive the test. It suggests something that has been rejected after testing
because it has failed to reach the required standard.
From the context it is clear that Paul has in view being rejected for the coveted prize, not being disqualified from entering the race. He will fail to win it if he
fails to comply with all the rules of the contest.

Paul appears to view himself in a dual role. He is
both competitor and herald of the lists. It was the
herald's function to announce the rules of the game
and to call out the competitors. The word *preached*
is derived from the verb "to herald." It was Paul's
fear that after having acted as a herald who bids others enter the contest, he himself should fail when
tested by the same standards. In such case, his exalted

position as a herald would only serve to aggravate the possible disgrace.

It should be noted that the failure he has in view stems from the body, and to guard against it he practiced rigorous self-discipline. Charles Hodge affirms that in Scripture the body as "the seat and organ of sin, is used of our whole sinful nature. It was not merely his sensual nature Paul endeavoured to bring into subjection, but all the evil propensities of his heart."

The panacea for this ever-present peril Paul conceived to lie not merely in the realm of doctrine or ethics but in the physical realm. The word *temperate* signifies self-mastered moderation—neither asceticism on the one hand nor self-indulgence on the other. He was not prepared to allow his body to become master, whether through appetite or lax indulgence. The clause "I bring it into subjection" pictures the victorious general leading home in his triumphal march those whom he has vanquished in battle and are now his slaves. A. S. Way appropriately renders this passage: "I browbeat my own animal nature, and treat it not as my master but my slave."

NOTES

1. Robert Louis Stevenson, in *The Reaper,* July 1942, p. 96.
2. Bishop Stephen Neill, in *The Record,* 28 March 1947, p. 161.
3. Helmut Thielecke, *Encounter with Spurgeon* (Philadelphia: Fortress, 1963).
4. J. R. Andrews, *George Whitefield* (London: Morgan & Scott, 1915), p. 412.
5. W. Y. Fullerton, *F. B. Meyer* (London: Marshall, Morgan & Scott, n.d.), p. 172.

6. Thielecke, p. 219.
7. N. G. Dunning, *Samuel Chadwick* (London: Hodder & Stoughton, 1934), p. 206.
8. H. C. A. Dixon, *A. C. Dixon* (New York: Putnam's, 1931), p. 277.
9. Ibid., p. 158.

22

NEHEMIAH, AN EXEMPLARY LEADER

Remember me, O my God, for good.

NEHEMIAH 13:31

One of the most striking biblical examples of inspiring and authoritative leadership is seen in the life of Nehemiah. At times his methods seemed somewhat vigorous, but he was used by God to achieve spectacular reforms in the life of his nation in an amazingly short time. An analysis of his personality and methods discloses that the methods he adopted were effective only because of the quality of his own character.

HIS CHARACTER

The first impression gained from reading his artless story is that he was a man of *prayer*. His first reaction on hearing of the pitiable plight of Jerusalem was to turn to God in prayer, evidence that he was no stranger at the throne of grace. Throughout, the record is liberally sprinkled with ejaculatory prayers. To him prayer was not merely an exercise for set seasons but an integral part of ordinary living and working (1:4, 6; 2:4; 4:4, 9; 5:19; 6:14; 13:14, 22, 29).

He displayed *courage* in the face of great danger. "Should a man like me flee? And could one such as I go into the temple to save his life? I will not go in" (6:11). That display of firmness and fearlessness would do much to increase the morale of a discouraged people.

He manifested *genuine concern* for the welfare of the people, a concern so obvious that even his adversaries commented on it. "It was very displeasing to them that someone had come to seek the welfare of the sons of Israel" (2:10). His concern found expression in fasting and prayers and tears (1:4-6). Nehemiah identified himself with his people, not only in their sorrows but also in their sins: "The sins of the sons of Israel, which *we* have sinned against Thee; I and my father's house have sinned" (1:6, italics added).

He exhibited keen *foresight*. Having secured the favorable attention of the king, he asked for letters to the governors through whose territories he was to travel. But his thoughts ranged further to the task awaiting him in Jerusalem, and he requested also letters to the keeper of the king's forests, so that he might obtain the timber necessary "to make beams for the gates of the fortress . . . for the wall of the city" (2:8). He thought things through carefully.

There was a strain of wholesome *caution* running

through Nehemiah's venturesome activities. On reaching Jerusalem, he did not precipitately embark upon his work. "So I came to Jerusalem and was there three days" (2:11). Only after that lapse of time, during which he had been carefully appraising the situation, did he act. And even then his innate caution caused him to maintain silence as to the purpose of his coming. Even his reconnaissance was done under cover of night.

Nehemiah was essentially a man of *clear decision.* He did not defer when he should decide. Procrastination found no place in his energetic nature.

He possessed the quality of *empathy* to an unusual degree. He was willing to lend an understanding and sympathetic ear to the problems and grievances of the people, and took remedial action (4:10-12; 5:1-5). (A leader remarked concerning one of his subordinates, "I was not going to have him weeping on my shoulder!" But that is what the leader's shoulder is for!)

Nehemiah's decisions and actions were characterized by *strict impartiality.* He manifested no respect of persons. The nobles and rulers received his censure when they deserved it just as freely as did the common people. "I contended with the nobles, and the rulers. . . . And I held a great assembly against them" (5:7).

His spiritual approach to problems did not exclude a *healthy realism.* "We prayed to our God . . . and set up a guard . . . day and night" (4:9).

In *accepting responsibility,* he did not evade its more onerous implications but was prepared to carry his assignment, with all its attendant difficulties, right through to a successful conclusion.

Nehemiah emerges as a man who was vigorous in administration, calm in crisis, fearless in danger, courageous in decision, thorough in organization, disinterested in leadership, persevering before opposition, resolute in the face of threats, vigilant against intrigue— a leader who won and held the full confidence of his followers.

HIS METHODS

He raised the morale of his colleagues. That is an important function of the responsible leader. He achieved that end by stimulating their faith and directing their thoughts away from the magnitude of their immediate problems to the greatness and trustworthiness of God. Scattered throughout the record are such assurances as these:

"The God of heaven . . . will give us success" (2:20).

"The joy of the LORD is your strength" (8:10).

Faith begets faith. Pessimism begets unbelief. It is a primary responsibility of the spiritual leader to feed faith to his colleagues.

He was generous in appreciation and encouragement. Nehemiah came to a discouraged and demoralized people. His first aim was to kindle hope and then to secure their cooperation. That he did in part by recounting the good hand of God, which had been on him, and sharing with them his vision and utter confidence in God. "I told them how the hand of my God had been favorable to me, and also about the king's words which he had spoken to me. Then they said, 'Let us arise and build.' So they put their hands to the good work" (2:18).

Faults and failings must be faithfully corrected, but it is the manner in which that is done that is important. Nehemiah appeared to be able to do it in such a way as to inspire the people to do better. More than that, his faithful and firm discipline won him continued confidence and further established his authority.

He dealt promptly with potential causes of weakness. Two typical cases are recorded.

The people were *discouraged through weariness and obstruction* (4:10-16). They were utterly tired; accumulated rubbish impeded their progress; their adversaries were intimidating them. What tactics did Nehemiah employ? He directed their thoughts to God. He saw to it that they were properly armed. He regrouped them and stationed them at strategic points. He harnessed the strengths of the family unit. He ordered half of them to work while the other half defended and rested. Courage returned to the people when they saw that their leader appreciated and was grappling with their problems.

In the second case the people were *disillusioned through greed and heartlessness* on the part of their rich brethren (5:1-5). Their lands were mortgaged; some of their children had been sold into slavery. "Neither is it in our power to redeem them; for other men have our lands and vineyards" (KJV). Nothing lowers the morale of people more than when the welfare of their children is adversely affected.

Again the tactics employed by Nehemiah are full of instruction. He listened attentively to their complaints and sympathized with them in their dilemma. He rebuked and shamed the nobles for their heartlessness in exacting harsh usury from their kinsmen (5:7). He contrasted their actions with his own altruism (5:14). He appealed for immediate restitution (5:11). So great was his spiritual ascendancy that they replied: "We will give it back, and will require nothing from them; we will do exactly as you say" (5:12).

Nehemiah restored the authority of the Word of God (8:1-8). The reforms that he instituted would have been short-lived or even impossible apart from that. He vigorously enforced the standards of the Word of God, and it imparted spiritual authority to his actions.

He ordered the restoration of the Feast of Tabernacles, which had not been observed since Joshua's day (8:14). How the work-weary people would welcome that week's holiday and festivities! The reading of the Scriptures induced repentance and confession of sin on the part of both people and priests (9:3-5). They cleansed the Temple of Tobiah's sacrilegious furniture (13:4-9). The holy vessels were restored (13:9), and tithes were once again brought to the treasury (13:5). The Sabbath rest was again enforced (13:15), intermarriage with the surrounding nations forbidden (13:23-25), and separation from them effected (13:30).

He was skillful in organization. Before making detailed plans he conducted a careful survey and made an objective appraisal of the situation (2:11-16). He made a detailed assessment of the personnel available. He did not neglect unglamorous paper work. Each group was entrusted with a specific and clearly defined area of responsibility. He gave adequate recognition to subordinate leaders, mentioning them by name and the place where each worked. They were given a sense that they were more than mere cogs in a machine. He practiced a wise delegation of responsibility. "I put Hanani my brother, and Hananiah the commander of the fortress, in charge over Jerusalem" (7:2). He was thus giving other able men the opportunity to develop their leadership potential. He had high standards for the subordinates whom he chose (7:2)—faithfulness, "he was a faithful man," and unusual piety, "he feared God more than many."

His leadership was demonstrated in *his attitude to organized opposition,* which took varied forms—insult, innuendo, infiltration, intimidation, and intrigue. It required wise and resolute guidance to steer a steady course amid those swirling currents.

Again his first recourse was to prayer. "We made our prayer unto our God" (4:9). When it was safe to do so, he simply ignored the adversaries. He steadfastly refused to allow them to deflect him from his central task, but at the same time he took all necessary precautionary measures (4:16). Most important of all, he never deviated from an attitude of unwavering faith in God (4:20).

The test of spiritual leadership is whether it results in the successful achievement of its objective. In the case of Nehemiah, that is not left in doubt. The record stands:

"So the wall was completed" (6:15).

SCRIPTURE INDEX

INDEX OF PERSONS

Take 5 part 3
three reminders
truth for life

The role of
a
Godly husband
pt 2